LITHOGRAPHY'S FIRST HALF CENTURY: THE AGE OF GOYA AND DELACROIX

Artists' Lithographs in Europe: 1801–1851

Department of Prints, Drawings, and Photographs

MUSEUM OF FINE ARTS, BOSTON
Trustman Galleries
January 10–July 7, 1996

ACKNOWLEDGMENTS

This exhibition is indebted to an earlier and much more extensive exhibition of lithography organized by Henry P. Rossiter for the Museum of Fine Arts in 1937: *An Exhibition of Lithographs, 527 Examples by 312 Different Artists from 1799 to 1937*. It is also deeply indebted to the department's various donors and endowed funds, particularly W. G. Russell Allen's extraordinary collection of early lithography and the Katherine E. Bullard Fund in Memory of Francis Bullard, which made possible the purchase of the Calabi Collection. The present catalogue was supported by the George Peabody Gardner Fund.

✧ ✧ ✧ ✧ ✧

This exhibition was selected and organized by Clifford S. Ackley, Sue Welsh Reed, and Anne Havinga of the Department of Prints, Drawings and Photographs. They were assisted by two volunteer summer interns, Alison Matthews and Dorien Wijstma, and by volunteer department assistant Paige Hamilton. Joanne Donovan of the Museum's William Morris Hunt Memorial Library arranged for necessary interlibrary loans. A considerable number of lithographs were conserved in preparation for the exhibition by Annette Manick and Alison Luxner of the Paper Conservation Laboratory under the direction of Roy Perkinson. The exhibition was matted and framed by Gail English. Brent Benjamin, deputy director for curatorial affairs and collections, provided essential support.

Library of Congress catalogue card no. 95-82065
ISBN 0-87846-433-6

Edited by Cynthia M. Purvis
Designed by Janet O'Donoghue
Printed by The Stinehour Press, Lunenburg, Vermont

LITHOGRAPHY'S FIRST HALF CENTURY: THE AGE OF GOYA AND DELACROIX

TWO HUNDRED YEARS AGO, from 1796 to 1798, the South German playwright and actor Aloys Senefelder (1771–1834), hoping to find a cheaper way of reproducing his plays, invented in Munich a revolutionary method of printing and printmaking, lithography or "chemical printing." Senefelder, who turned out to be far more creative as an inventor than as a dramatist, continued to refine his invention and explore various aspects of it until the end of his life. Although Senefelder himself was not an artist and the invention was first applied to practical ends such as the reproducing of music scores, it was not long before artists were encouraged to experiment with this new means of multiplying original images. This exhibition celebrates Senefelder's invention by presenting a selective survey of the first fifty years of lithographs produced by European and British artists, from 1801 to 1851.

A second stimulus for the exhibition was provided by the Museum of Fine Arts' 1995 acquisition of the Augusto Calabi Collection of early Italian lithographs. The exhibition provides a first opportunity to see some of the most expressive of these little-known Italian images in the context of early artists' lithographs from other European schools.

Based exclusively on the Museum's permanent collection, including books illustrated with artists' lithographs, the exhibition does not pretend to completeness but nevertheless encompasses, in highly concentrated form, a wide spectrum of imagery and ways of using the lithographic medium. The exhibition is arranged thematically for comparison and contrast of treatment of subject, style, and technique rather than by chronology or national schools. The checklist at the end of the publication reproduces the installation sequence of the exhibition.

✧ ✧ ✧ ✧ ✧

LITHOGRAPHY IS BASED ON A SIMPLE CHEMICAL PRINCIPAL: grease attracts grease and water repels it. A greasy mark made with crayon or lithographic ink on a limestone slab polished to greater or lesser degree of fineness attracts the greasy printer's ink when the stone is inked. The stone is kept damp during inking and printing so that water repels the greasy ink from the untouched, and therefore blank, areas of the stone. The printing surface is perfectly level, or plane; the process does not involve raising or lowering the surface that receives the ink as in woodcut or engraving and etching. Senefelder did not, however, arrive immediately at what we regard today as the classic lithographic process (chemical printing). In 1796 he was already printing from Bavarian limestone slabs, but was etching them into relief to be printed like a block print or, subsequently, etching and engraving them like an intaglio plate. It was apparently not until 1798 that lithography as we know it was finally developed, through trial and error and happy accident. In 1799 Senefelder received a patent from the Bavarian government for the process.

The new process naturally aroused enormous curiosity, and lithographic presses were soon set up not only in Munich but throughout Germany. In the first decade of the nineteenth century lithography was introduced into several other countries, among them England (1800–01), France (1801–02), and Italy (1805–07). These years also see the beginning of artists' creative use of lithography. A key point of diffusion for lithography was the music publishing firm of Johann Anton André in Offenbach, Germany. In 1799 André paid Senefelder a fee to explain the process to him and to help him set up lithographic presses in Offenbach. In 1800, Senefelder accompanied André's brother, Friedrich, to London, where they had been preceded by another André brother, Philipp. The latter received a patent in 1801 and began to send stones and lithographic ink to prominent artists such as the American-born Benjamin West, then president of London's Royal Academy, asking them to try their hand in the new medium (no. 48, pl. 22). In 1803, twelve of these original artists' lithographs were issued by Philipp André under the title *Specimens of Polyautography*. Six of the prints that appeared in that publication are included in this exhibition.

"Polyautography" (literally: multiple original handwriting) was one of the many names, including *Steindruck,* or stone-printing, under which the new printing process was known until the French term lithography (*lithographie,* literally "stone writing") gained in popularity from 1805 on. The 1803 title page for *Specimens,* which shows an infant winged genius, armed with ink and pen, calligraphing the text onto a giant lithographic stone embedded in greenery, underlines the overtones of artistic originality inherent in the term "polyautography" by speaking of "Impressions taken from Original Drawings." The term "lithography" was finally adopted by Senefelder himself when he published a treatise on his process in German, French, and English in 1818–19.

In 1806 J.G. Vollweiler, Philipp André's London successor, completed the project André had begun by re-issuing the first twelve *Specimens* prints plus twenty-four more for a total of thirty-six lithographs by thirty different artists. Although artistically of considerable interest, the *Specimens* project was not a commercial success and both André and Vollweiler returned to Germany. In Germany itself, the Berlin artist Wilhelm Reuter, who had made original lithographs as early as 1801, issued from 1804 to 1807 his own series of *Polyautographic Drawings by Outstanding Berlin Artists,* followed by a second, more ambitious and never completed series of 1818, *Polyautographic Drawings by the Most Outstanding European Artists of Our Time*. Ludwig Wolf's *Hero and Leander* (no. 49), was to be number one in the projected series.

Lithography was introduced into France by Friedrich André in 1801–02. A few rare early artistic successes with lithography date from this first decade, particularly the works of the classicizing artist Pierre Nolasque Bergeret from 1804–05 (nos. 7, 45, pl. 30), but commercial applications of the process such as music sheet covers were more common at the time. Artistic lithography, which was to flourish in early nineteenth-century France as in no other country, did not firmly take root, however, until 1815–16 when Charles de Lasteyrie and Godefroy Engelmann (soon followed by other significant artistic printers such as François Delpech and Charles Motte) set up their presses in Paris. Certain prominent figures of the Napoleonic era had visited Munich in order to try their hand at lithography. Among them were the gifted amateurs General Louis François Lejeune, whose mounted *Cossack* of 1806 (no. 92) initiates the whole genre of Napoleonic military imagery in French lithography, and in 1809, Dominique Vivant Denon, Napoleon's minister of fine arts (no. 98), who was to become an enthusiastic advocate of lithography. On the whole, however, the political unrest of the Napoleonic years held back the advance of artistic lithography.

In 1816, then-celebrated Neo-classical artists such as Anne Louis Girodet-Trioson (nos. 19, 44, pl. 31) and Pierre Narcisse Guérin (no. 101, pl. 34) produced elegantly drawn and skillfully printed lithographs with printers such as Engelmann in order to demonstrate to the Parisian art bureaucracy the artistic viability of the medium. Théodore Géricault, who took up lithography in 1817, had by 1818 produced the first unqualified masterpieces in the new medium, works such as the *Boxers* (no. 75, pl. 53) and the *Wagon Loaded with Wounded Soldiers* (no. 83, pl. 17), the latter one of the most powerful and least sentimental of an immense outpouring of nostalgic Napoleonic military imagery produced after the fall of Napoleon and the restoration of the monarchy.

The first Italian artists' lithographs were printed in Rome in 1805 by printers from Munich. In 1807, the publisher G. De Werz (or Werz) from Munich and his printer, Grünewald, set up shop in Milan. The years 1808–12 in Milan were ones of artistic experimentation with the medium. Although probably no more commercially successful than the first artists' lithographs produced in London, Berlin or Paris, a few Milanese works of great subtlety and beauty survive in a small number of impressions. These paved the way for the dominant figure of early Italian lithography (active in Milan), Francesco Hayez, protégé of the celebrated sculptor Antonio Canova.

Senefelder's published treatise of 1818 (French and English translations, 1819) reveals his fertility of invention and anticipates future developments. He describes printing with several colors, which achieved its first artistically satisfying expression in Thomas Shotter Boys' series of city views of 1839 (no. 9). He also describes the "sprinkled manner," or use of spatter effects, which would come into its own in the 1880s and 90s in the hands of the French artists Jules Chéret and Henri de Toulouse-Lautrec, and is to be seen here in the floating ashes of Cesare di Benevello's raging forest fire (no. 61, pl. 43). Senefelder's recognition of the need to find more convenient alternatives to the weighty, brittle lithographic stones is evident in his description of transfer paper on which the artist could draw and then transfer the image to the stone; his invention of easily portable paper "stones" with a special coating (here employed for Géricault's English pen lithograph, *The Sleeping Fish Merchant* of 1820, no. 11, pl. 9); and his description of printing lithographically from metal plates.

Much of Senefelder's treatise is, however, surprisingly preoccupied with the imitation of older printmaking techniques such as woodcut, engraving and etching. It is a classic observation that, in the first years after the introduction of a new method of printing or graphic reproduction, a great deal of energy is often expended in the emulation of what has gone before rather than in developing a new vocabulary for a new medium. Such use of an older visual vocabulary is evident here in a number of early lithographs that derive their linear systems of cross-hatching or stipple from those of professional engraving and etching.

An allegory of the invention of lithography is seen in the classicizing artist N.H. Jacob's 1819 lithograph from the portfolio of plates accompanying the French edition of Senefelder's treatise (no. 4, pl. 1) The winged youthful nude genius of lithography's invention is assisted by an attendant muse in empire dress who pulls from a carefully labeled "Bavarian stone" on the bed of the press a lithograph listing the names of various early artistic practitioners of the medium, including many represented here: the Vernets, Quaglio, Isabey, Marlet, Bourgeois, etc. The genius clutches in his hand a holder with sharpened litho crayons and, in the foreground, one sees the inking roller resting on its slab. The execution of the print, although it innovatively makes use of washes of lithographic ink as well as crayon, is suave, mannered, highly finished, and still somewhat evocative of the vocabulary of professional engraving and etching.

A contrast in graphic vocabulary is offered by the great caricaturist Honoré Daumier's freely crayoned 1840 vignette of two men eagerly reading the satirical journal *Le Charivari*, a lithograph cut from the pages of that journal (no. 8, pl. 2). Daumier's direct handling of lithography suggests the scribbling speed and freedom latent in the medium and reminds one of the urgency of journalistic deadlines.

The principal subject of a number of the French images in the exhibition is the market for lithographs. Bergeret's pioneering 1804 image of the caricature publisher Martinet's shop shows a crowd of living caricatures of current fashion gawking at caricatures of themselves displayed in Martinet's window (no. 7). This hand-colored pen lithograph is barely recognizable as a lithograph, being closely based on the hand-colored line etchings that preceded it. Carle Vernet's crayon lithograph of the street front of Delpech's shop (no. 6) shows a young apprentice or messenger transporting one of the heavy lithographic stones, which rests on a pad on his head. In Nicolas Toussaint Charlet's lithograph of a humble book-stall that sells lithographs, a Napoleonic veteran points out to a younger soldier Napoleonic battle scenes of the sort that Charlet himself produced in such quantity (no. 5, pl. 3).

Lithographs, which could be printed relatively cheaply and easily in large editions, provide us with a wide-ranging documentation of the life of the times, whether in the form of charged political images such as those Daumier produced for Charles Philipon, the Parisian publisher of the controversial journal of political satire, *La Caricature* (as well as the later and milder, more socially satirical journal, *Le Charivari*), or scenes of street life, whether mundane or monumental, by Géricault (nos. 11, 12; pls. 9, 12). In Louis Lecoeur's ironic slice of street life from about 1815, *The Plaything of the Moment* (no. 16 , pl. 6), a self-satisfied provincial dandy, togged out in the latest fashion, assumes (as the verses printed below the image inform us) that an elegantly dressed young woman is ogling him through a spy-glass when, in fact, she is engrossed in the latest novelty, a kaleidoscope. The pleading beggars are ignored by both.

After the fall of Napoleon and the restoration of the monarchy, publishers of Republican sympathies such as Philipon began to heckle and snipe at the government. Decamp's 1830 satire on the recently deposed Charles X, a mock entry from a future court circular, mercilessly ridicules the impotence and futility of the royal house by presenting the Royal Hunt as the pot-shots taken by a senile monarch, ensconced in the comfort of an armchair, at a toy rabbit pulled by a lackey (no. 14, pl. 18). At the opposite pole, Restoration propaganda at its most seductive is seen in Jean Baptiste Isabey's delicately executed, soft-focus 1821 lithograph in which the infant Duc de Bordeaux (his father, heir to the throne, had been assassinated the year before) is triumphantly greeted by the local populace as he arrives at the Chateau of Chambord, the whole enveloped in a silvery haze of glory (no. 17, pl. 10).

It was Charles X's successor, Louis Philippe, who—until absolute censorship was finally imposed in 1835—was most savagely attacked by the Republican image-sellers. Philipon received so many heavy fines for his publications' transgressions that he founded a Monthly Association for the Freedom of the Press in order to raise some money. Subscribers received large lithographic caricatures suitable for framing, including Daumier's mass character assassination of legislators and government, the *Legislative Belly,* a study in swelling rotundities in which each head was based on a previous study in sculpture (no. 18). The last lithograph published by the Association was Daumier's devastating study in modern realism that documents a government reprisal against innocent civilians in a working class quarter, *Rue Transnonain, 15 April, 1834* (no. 15). As Philipon wrote with inflammatory rhetoric: "It's not a caricature . . . it's a bloody page from our modern history." In Daumier's print, the slain—powerfully modeled and dramatized by bold patterns of light and shadow—are at once shockingly real and monumentally heroic: a dead worker in a nightshirt evokes a martyr in a Renaissance painting. Philipon even enlisted the help of a Romantic landscape painter, Paul Huet, when he wished to convey more effectively, and morbidly, his bitingly ironic idea for a political cartoon: *Full and Total Amnesty Granted by Death in 1832* (no. 13, pl. 19), a cemetery full of the carefully labeled tombstones of those who had perished as political prisoners in that year.

Lithography was responsible for an explosion of inventive portraiture, from the exquisite miniaturistic delicacy and lightness of the anonymous Milanese portrait of Napoleon's empress Marie Louise (no. 25, pl. 20) to the cellar light, oppressive shadows, and high-strung melancholy of Eugène Delacroix's heavily crayoned 1826 portrait of his German painter friend, Baron Schwiter (no. 30, pl. 21). Self-portraits are legion: they range from J. D. Odevaere's (a Belgian pupil of J. L. David) pompously official, decorations-and-all, self-image of 1816 (no. 26, pl. 4), in which he holds a thin lithographic stone on which he is drawing his portrait, to portraitist and fashion illustrator Achille Devéria's modishly demonic and bohemian 1830 portrait "with the fatal look," in which he has his crayon-holder poised and ready (no. 29, pl. 5).

A central feature of early nineteenth-century art was the illustration of biblical, mythological, or literary texts, as in Benjamin West's flamboyant lithographic pen sketch of 1801 representing the angel of the Resurrection at Christ's tomb (no. 48, pl. 22) or Girodet-Trioson's subtly modeled, silvery moonlit crayon lithograph of 1816 (no. 44, pl. 31), a scene of deluge and disaster from that sensationally successful eighteenth-century literary forgery by the Scottish poet Macpherson, the epic poems of Ossian, the imaginary "ancient Celtic bard."

French and Italian artists such as Delacroix or Hayez were drawn to poems, novels, and plays set in earlier times or in exotic places, particularly works by foreign writers such as Goethe, Shakespeare or Sir Walter Scott that lent themselves to non-classical scenes of strong emotion, violent action, or supernatural terror in a picturesque setting. The epitome of such works are Delacroix's highly original illustrations to Goethe's *Faust* published in 1828 (no. 34, pl. 23). Violently exaggerated in the drawing—almost to the point of caricature—in order to more powerfully convey heightened sensations, these works take full advantage of the rich modulation of dark tones the lithographic crayon is capable of. Scraping out lights with a sharp point lends an electrical charge to one horse's mane as Faust and Mephistopheles madly gallop to the witches' Sabbath. The intimate relationship between literature and art in Delacroix's work is illuminated by a passage introducing his 1829 illustration representing the ancient Gallic king, Vercingétorix (no. 52) in which Delacroix is praised as "the Byron, the Victor Hugo of his art." Delacroix's later works show no less sensitivity to tone, but the drawing becomes more balanced and poised, less prone to near-hysterical exaggeration. In his 1843 image of Hamlet seeing his father's ghost (no. 31), the moon-drenched battlements set the uncanny mood but the drawing of the figures is more controlled and contained.

Unlike the *Faust* illustrations, Delacroix's 1834–43 *Hamlet* plates are a series of "scenes from," rather than illustrations inserted into, a printed text. The latter is also true for Hayez's large-format, incomplete series of scenes from Tommaso Grossi's epic poem about the Lombards in the Crusades (no. 33), or his published series of scenes from Sir Walter Scott's novel set in the Crusades, *Ivanhoe* (no. 32, pl. 24). The earlier illustration to Grossi's poem is rendered in a lighter-toned, open style with a rhythmic undulation of contour that calls attention to the drawn line, while the later *Ivanhoe* illustrations are rendered in a highly polished "painting with lithographic crayons" style that stresses fullness of tonal range, specificity of detail, and overall finish.

Artists not only illustrated pre-existing texts, ancient and modern, they also invented imaginary scenes, figures, and portrait heads that have a literary or anecdotal flavor. Bergeret's classically spare and geometric 1804–05 *Deathbed Scene in Antiquity* (no. 45, pl. 30), for example, evokes Greek vase painting and the Neo-classical vogue for outline illustration. In Berlin painter Menzel's 1851 scene of swashbuckling seventeenth-century swordplay on a spiral staircase, *The Pursuit*, washes of lithographic ink, scraping, and a warm colored tint stone summon up flickering lights and shadows (no. 36). Pierre Paul Prud'hon's highly mannered and stylized, voluptuous woman reader clearly swoons from an excess of romantic emotion induced by her reading (no. 42, pl. 25), but the situation in Francisco Goya's freely sketched lithograph of a woman, eyes closed, her head resting in an older woman's lap—while other women look on with concern— is more mysterious: is she asleep, dreaming, or under a spell (no. 37, pl. 26) ? This is one of twelve experimental lithographs of modest format, printed in very small numbers, that Goya made in the period 1819–26 (see also no. 95, pl. 14).

Imaginary or fantasy portrait heads include English artist James Barry's imposing 1803 pen lithograph of a Lear-like "eastern patriarch" with a view of distant ruins (no. 50); Italian artist Andrea Appiani's 1808–12 crayon lithograph, printed in brownish ink, of a bearded man who resembles an antique bust that has found life and speech (no. 106, pl. 36); and Berlin artist Wilhelm Reuter's vaporous, rapidly sketched 1818 crayon profile of a Christ-like bearded man printed on paper prepared with yellowish watercolor (no. 103, pl. 37).

The Neo-classical world of figures of unearthly purity that appear sculpted from white marble and drawn with exquisite clarity of line, is epitomized by Guérin's 1816, *The Vigilant One* (no. 101, pl. 34), an allegory of the industrious young artist who burns the midnight oil, fending off Sleep with her poppies as the sun rises and Love mourns, neglected, in a corner. This is one of three allegories of young artists executed by Guérin at this time; the others being "The one who takes on too much" and "The lazy one." Another, but very different, lamp-lit "antique scene" is represented by Daumier's *Penelope's Nights* from his hilarious series, *Histoire Ancienne,* in which heroes and heroines of antiquity and mythology such as Penelope, the notoriously faithful wife of the wandering Ulysses, are viewed through the jaundiced eye of modern realism (no. 100, pl. 35). Daumier's series of 1841–43 constitutes the ultimate revolt against the cult of the antique and classical learning: an introduction to the series refers with heavy irony to "Ingres and Daumier, those Siamese twins of beauty."

Lithography became a major means of conveying the early nineteenth century's preoccupation with travel and the picturesque, particularly the Romantic movement's fascination with medieval architecture. This was most dramatically expressed in the gargantuan multi-volume publication that was issued from 1820 to 1878, Baron Taylor's *Voyages pittoresques et romantiques dans l'ancienne France.* The publication involved large numbers of French and English artists and printers. Plates from the first volumes published in the 1820s are redolent of the Romantic movement in their dramatic and mysterious, highly evocative use of tonal effects (nos. 51, 52).

Many lithographic landscapes of the early nineteenth century have the double function of pictorially evoking the atmosphere and textures of the countryside while recording with topographic accuracy the features of a particular place or region; see, for example, Simon Warnberger's 1807 vista, *Around the Schlier-See* (no. 68), or M.J. Wagenbauer's 1808 view, *In the Vicinity of Wangen* (no. 69). The dialogue between the alternatives of pure outline and painterly tone is evident when one compares Théodore d'Aligny's light-filled pen lithograph of a rocky landscape of about 1835 (no. 66, pl. 44) with Eugène Isabey's small, but radical, painterly experiment with brush, ink, and scraper, the brooding *Stormy Weather* from the same decade (no. 65, pl. 46). An obsessive motif in landscape at this period, a theme that relates closely to the Romantic artist's notion of nature as alive, an ongoing process, is the ancient tree contorted or hollowed out by the struggle for existence; see, for example, Raphael Lamar West's 1802 *Ancient Oak with Seated Man* (no. 63) or Henry W. Burgess's *Two Trees in an Old Graveyard* of about 1815 (no. 71).

The struggle for existence, Nature "red in tooth and claw," a fascination with animal vitality and a preoccupation with the animal spirit in man, are all aspects of Romantic sensibility. These themes are vividly expressed in lithographs by Delacroix, Ward, Goya, Géricault, and others from the 1820s. Delacroix's *Frightened Wild Horse* (no. 76) is no less haunted than the English animal painter James Ward's portrait of equine overbreeding, Napoleon's captured charger, *Marengo*, spooked by the cry of a bird in a deserted moonlit moorland (no. 3, pl. 48). Ward's lithograph transcends the conventional English genre of the horse portrait by adding a psychological dimension. Delacroix's *Royal Tiger* is not only a masterpiece of tonal and textural description in which crayon, brush, and scraper discover the black and white equivalents for the texture and colors of painting, but also a study of the intensely alien nature of wild things (no. 1, pl. 49, see detail, cover). Awe or terror in the face of nature's untameable power is one of the essential themes of Romantic art. This is seen at its highest pitch in the ferocity of Delacroix's *Wild Horse Brought Down by a*

A NOTE ON THE CALABI COLLECTION

The Italian lithographs in this exhibition by Appiani, Hayez, Longhi, Sabatelli, and others were selected from a recently acquired collection—nearly 600 Italian, as well as 300 lithographs of other European schools. Many of these lithographs were collected from Italian printing establishments in the late nineteenth century by A. Gaffuri, a lithographic printer and collector, and were subsequently acquired by Augusto Calabi, a renowned print scholar. Calabi relied on the collection to write a book on Italian lithographs made before 1840, *Saggio sulla litografia, La prima produzione Italiana in rapporto a quella degli altri paesi sino al 1840* (Milan, 1958). The dating of the early Italian lithographs in this exhibition is based on Calabi's research as published in the foregoing volume. This acquisition has made the Museum of Fine Arts one of the only significant resources for the study of early Italian lithography outside of Italy.

Tiger, which is also an example of the wonderfully velvety textures that the scraper can evoke from a crayon-covered stone surface (no. 81, pl. 52).

Francisco Goya's lithographs of 1825, the four large bullfighting subjects executed in exile in Bordeaux at the end of his life, explore animal bravery and aggression in man and beast. The sense of dramatic struggle arises above all from the strikingly simple compositions, with their broad patches of deep tone and flashes of brilliant light, as well as from the incomparable breadth and energy with which crayon and scraper have been handled. Goya, in his first major etchings, the *Caprichos* of 1799, worked from dark to light, subtly scraping away areas of aquatint. He continues in the same fashion here, boldly scraping out or toning down whole passages as he changes his mind (nos. 77–80, pl. 50, see detail, cover). Italian artist Luigi Sabatelli's *The Bear Hunter* of about 1820 (no. 82, pl. 51) pits the herculean strength of the hunter against the ferocity of the cornered bear; he uses the scraper to make changes (in the position of the hunter's hand) or to add subtle definition and texture. Ritualized combat between man and man is cast into the mode of heroic sculpture in Géricault's *Boxers* (no. 75, pl. 53), a transformation of a familiar type of English sporting print. With a simple but inventive use of the medium, pen and lithographic ink describe the torso of the black pugilist and lithographic crayon that of the white boxer.

Overwhelming numbers of French lithographs representing Napoleonic military subjects were issued in this period. On the one hand, we have the brutal but heroic realism of Géricault's *Wagon Loaded with Wounded Soldiers* of 1818 (no. 83, pl. 17), in which the cart horses attacking each other reflect the savagery of war. On the other, we have the eerie ultra-romanticism of Auguste Marie Raffet's two lithographic fantasies in which Napoleon's legions are called back from the dead and pass in ghostly nocturnal review before their commander (nos. 87, 88). In Mongin's moody, operatic morality play, *The Duel,* two soldiers desert their duty and forfeit their lives in order to settle a personal quarrel while, in the far distance, the comrades they have abandoned are ambushed by the enemy (no. 86, pl. 16). Napoleon's Egyptian campaign encouraged an interest in exotic and Near Eastern subjects, particularly those dealing with the fiercely brave and loyal Egyptian warrior caste, the Mamelukes. Inevitably, many of these Napoleonic military and "Arab of the Desert" subjects focus on that creature of nervous temperament and barely controllable power, the horse: see, for example, horse painter Carle Vernet's lithograph of a Mameluke restraining a rearing horse (no. 89).

In principal, lithography did not require special skills of the artist, as did etching, engraving, or woodcut: all that was required was that the artist know how to draw. A skilled lithographic printer could do the rest. In the first years of experimentation this was apparently not always so. In England in 1801–03, for example, the artists working with Philipp André produced more pen lithographs than crayon lithographs. The printers were evidently less experienced with the printing of the granular broken tones of crayon lithographs as opposed to the unmodulated flat tones of images drawn with pen and lithographic ink. Pen lithographs were executed on highly polished stones that offered little resistance to the glide of the pen, while crayon lithographs were executed on more coarsely ground stones; the rougher texture, or tooth, produced the desired broken tones. Then again, the taste of the time may simply have favored the fluidity and graphic clarity of the pen lithographs.

After the first years, however, technical difficulties were rare. Therefore it is sometimes puzzling when later writers complain about the lack of tonal depth and range, the gray, washed-out qualities of certain early lithographs. What they are often, in fact, complaining about is not the printers' technical shortcomings, but the artists' conscious choices of style. Viewed from the perspective of the full, sonorous tonalities of Romantic lithography of the 1820s and later, it is sometimes difficult to fully appreciate the clarity, delicacy, and precision of lithographs by artists such as Ingres, Girodet, and Guérin that parallel the effects of marks made with a fine graphite pencil; or to fully empathize with works by artists such as J. B. Isabey and others who consciously strive for an ethereal silvery, middle-gray tone. To continually play off Neoclassical linear purity and marble pallor of tone against the rich shadowy tonal effects of Romanticism is, of course, a somewhat simplistic exercise because many artists partake of the qualities of both. But a consciousness of the ongoing dialogue between the two styles does offer valuable insight into issues of style and execution in artists' lithographs of this time.

Many of the earliest artists' lithographs, such as the first English pen lithographs or the earliest Milanese lithographs, have the character of sketch sheets or study sheets rather than finished works of art. In the case of the Milanese works, this impression was sometimes heightened by printing in grayish or brownish inks rather than black.

Additional tone, or a suggestion of color, was often achieved by devices such as the addition of a "tint stone" that printed continuous tone rather than line. In Domenico Quaglio's view of the tenth-century chapel in the castle at Nuremberg (no. 54), the tint stone strengthens the impression of candle-lit gloom and adds to the weightiness of the massive architecture. In Chassériau's lithograph of Venus freshly risen from the sea, the dark ivory tint stone adds to the sensuality of the goddess's figure by evoking creamy flesh tones (no. 43, pl. 29). Beginning in the 1820s, it became common to print lithographs on a thin sheet of fine paper that was mounted to a heavier backing sheet in the act of printing. This sheet provided a surface more receptive to the printing of the finer nuances of tone or detail and sometimes also provided an intermediate gray tone or suggestion of color. As frequently indicated in the foregoing text, subtraction of tone by scraping it away with a sharp point or a broad blade in order to make corrections or to add details, outlines, highlights, modeling, or texture, was frequently an important expressive tool of nineteenth-century lithographic artists, regardless of style.

Properly handled, lithography has a special ability to capture and replicate the immediacy and unique qualities—whether delicate and deliberate or bold and free—of the artist's personal gesture. This exhibition explores lithography's artistic beginnings and its first vigorous flowering, what might properly be called the golden age of black and white lithography, reflecting the artists' fresh sense of discovery and excitement about this wonderfully direct and easily accessible new means of producing multiple originals.

CLIFFORD S. ACKLEY
Ruth and Carl Shapiro Curator of Prints, Drawings, and Photographs

The following sources on early lithography were frequently consulted for this essay:

Farwell, Beatrice, *The Charged Image: French Lithographic Caricature 1816–1848*, Santa Barbara: Santa Barbara Museum of Art, 1989

Henker, Michael et al., *Von Senefelder zu Daumier: Die Anfänge der Lithographischen Kunst*, Haus der Bayerischen Geschichte, Veröffentlichungen zur Bayerischen Geschichte und Kultur, Nr. 16/88, Munich: K.G. Saur, 1988 (also available in a French edition)

Man, Felix H., *150 Years of Artists' Lithographs, 1803–1953*, London: William Heinemann Ltd., 1953

Man, Felix H., "Lithography in England (1801–1810)" in *Prints: Thirteen Illustrated Essays on the Art of the Print, Selected for the Print Council of America by Carl Zigrosser*, New York: Holt, Rinehart and Winston, 1962

Twyman, Michael, *Lithography, 1800–1850: The Techniques of Drawing on Stone in England and France and their Application in Works of Topography*, London: Oxford University Press, 1970

Weber, Wilhelm, *A History of Lithography*, New York: McGraw-Hill, 1966

Winkler, R. Arnim, *Die Frühzeit der deutschen Lithographie: Katalog der Bilddrucke von 1796–1821*, Materialien zur Kunst des 19. Jahrhunderts, Band 16, Munich: Prestel-Verlag, 1975

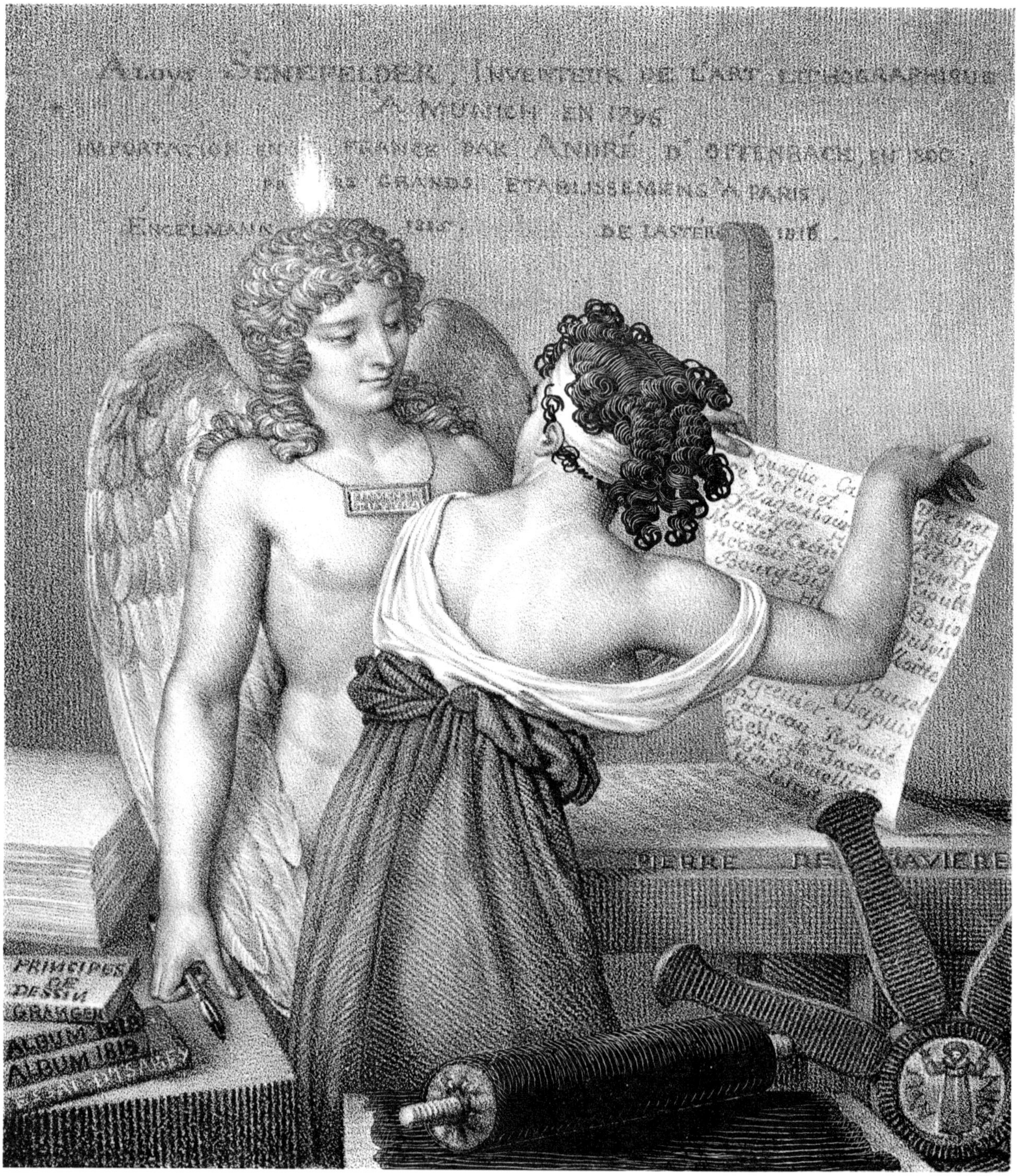

1. Nicolas Henri Jacob, *The Genius of the Invention of Lithography*, 1819 (cat. 4)

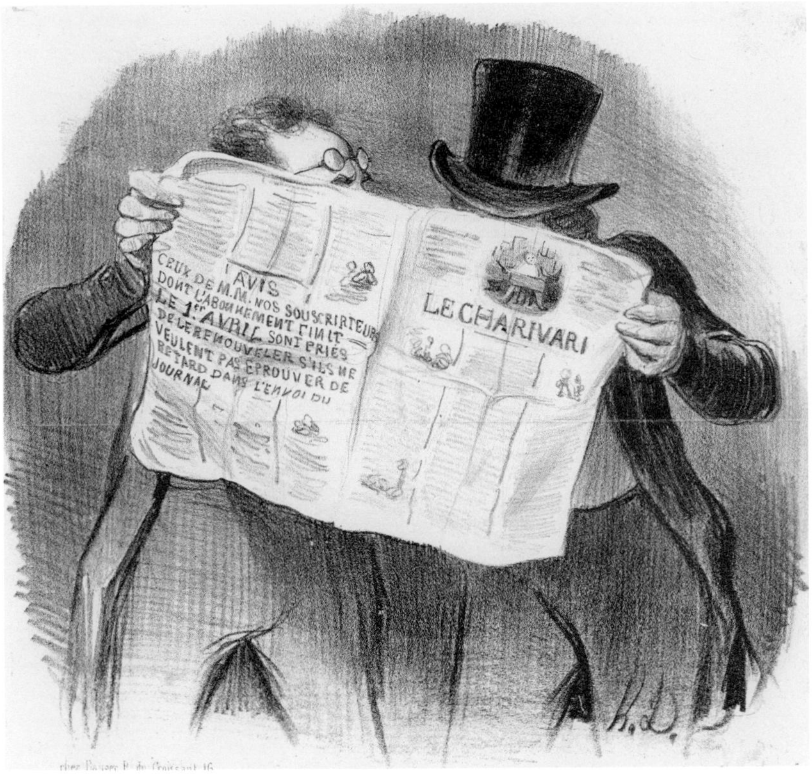

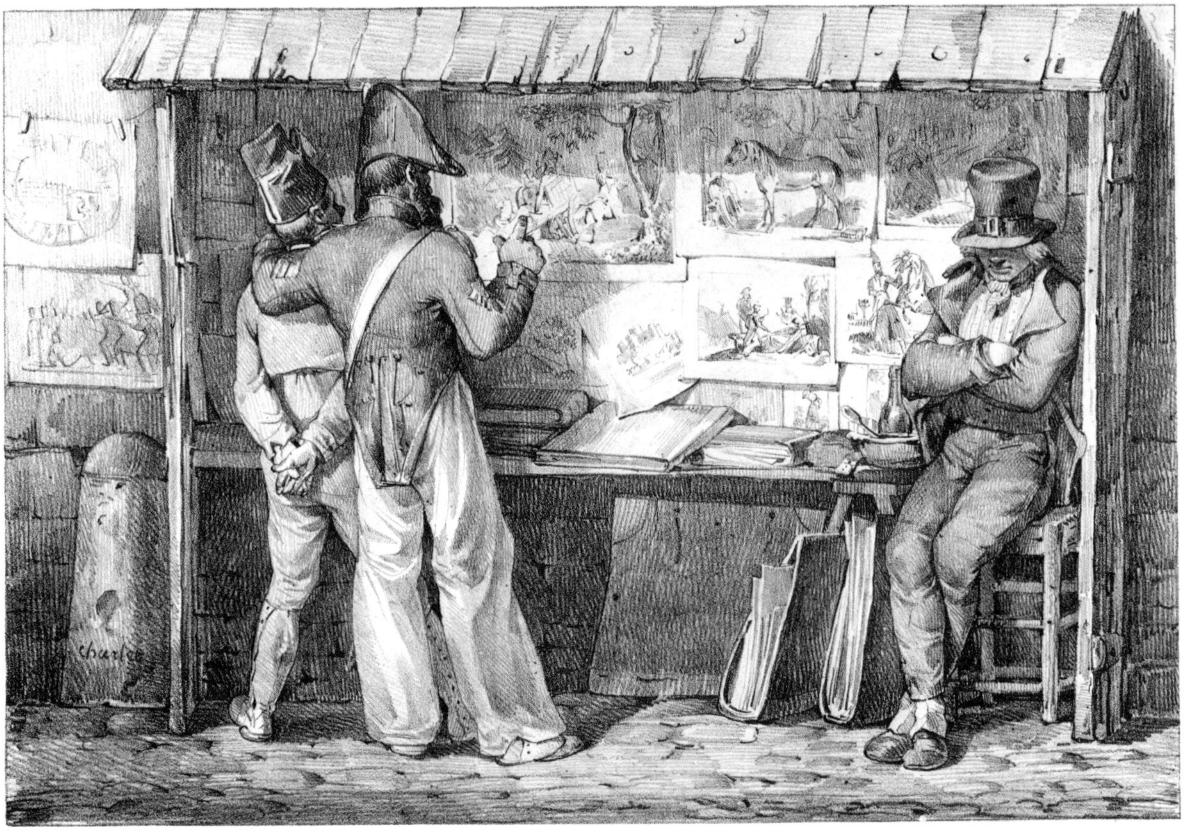

2. Honoré Daumier, *Two Men Reading* Le Charivari, 1840 (cat. 8)

3. Nicolas Toussaint Charlet, *The Seller of Lithographic Drawings*, about 1819 (cat. 5)

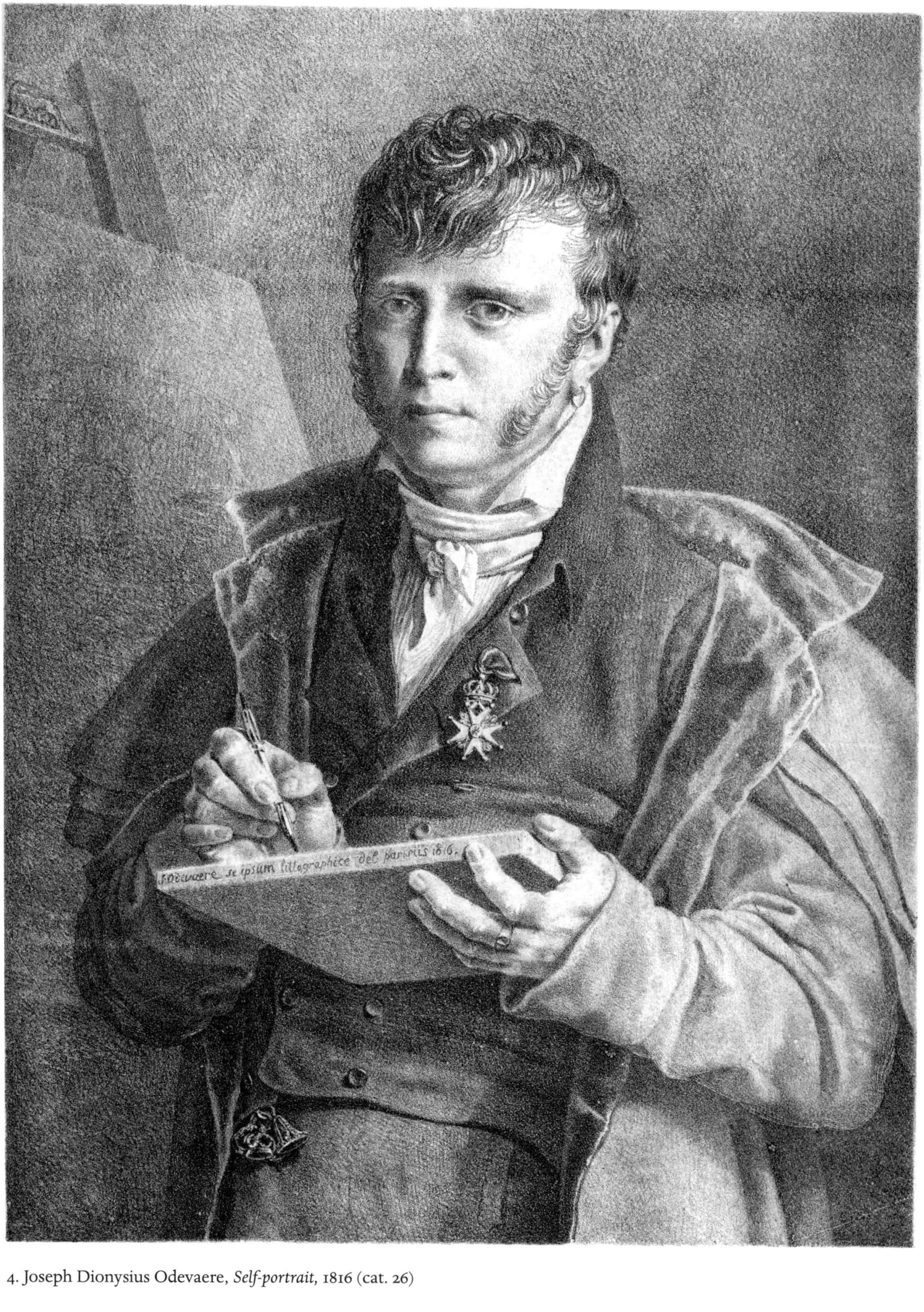

4. Joseph Dionysius Odevaere, *Self-portrait,* 1816 (cat. 26)

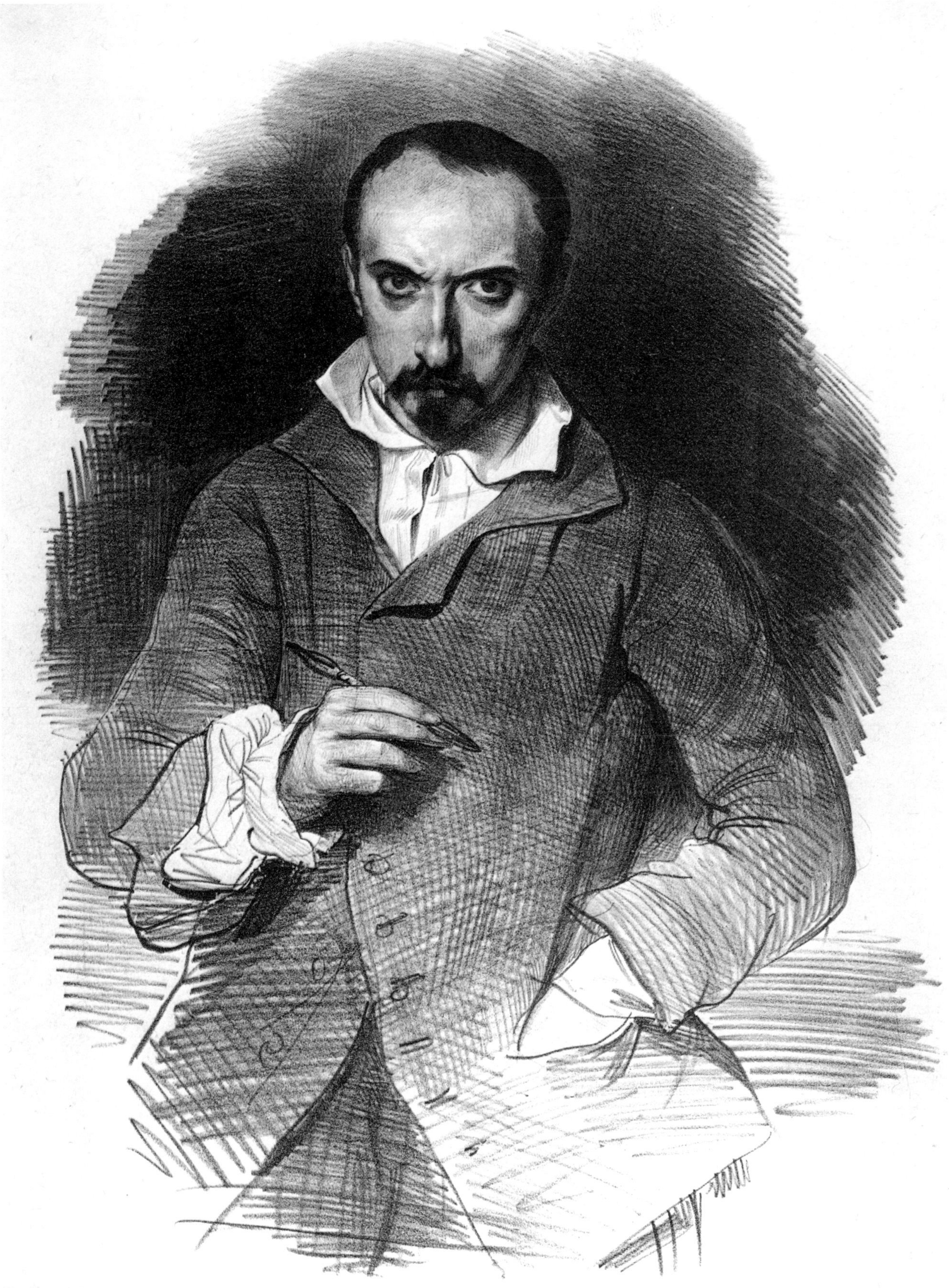

5. Achille Devéria, *Self-portrait,* 1830 (cat. 29)

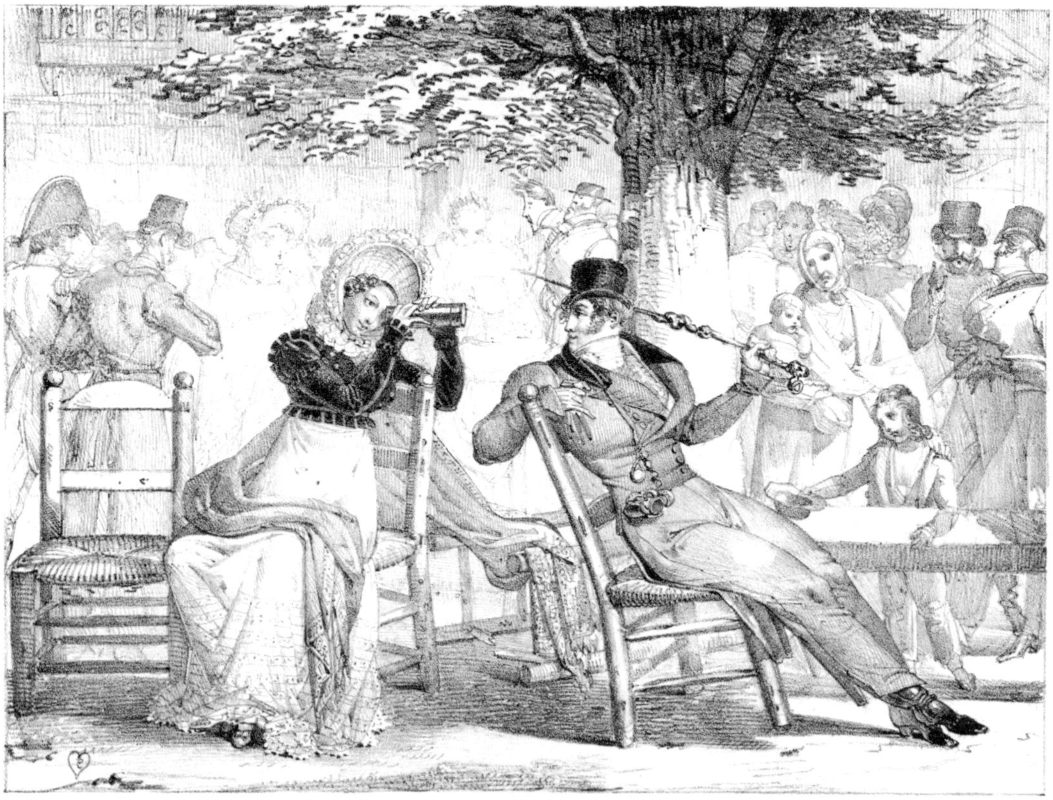

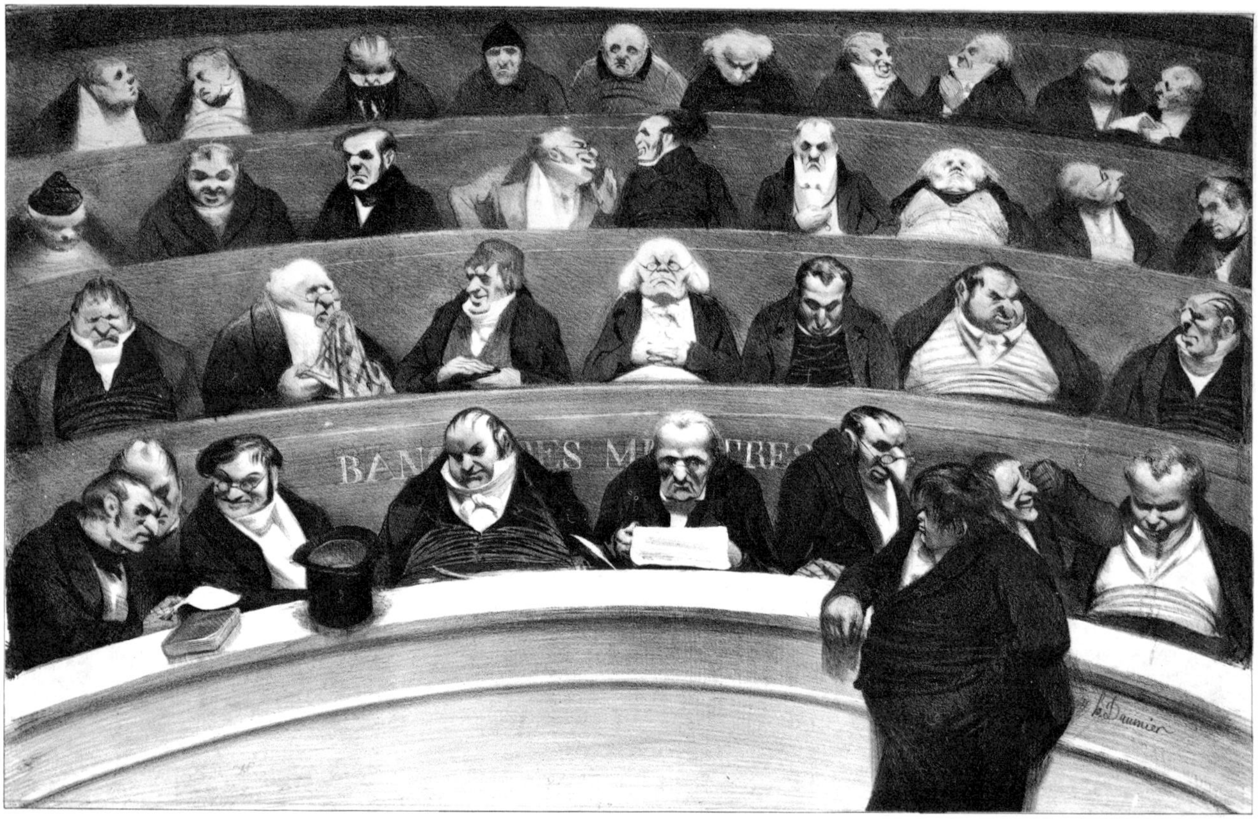

6. Louis Lecoeur, *The Plaything of the Moment*, about 1815 (cat. 16)

7. Honoré Daumier, *The Legislative Belly, View of the Ministers' Benches in the Unprostituted Chamber of 1834* (cat. 18)

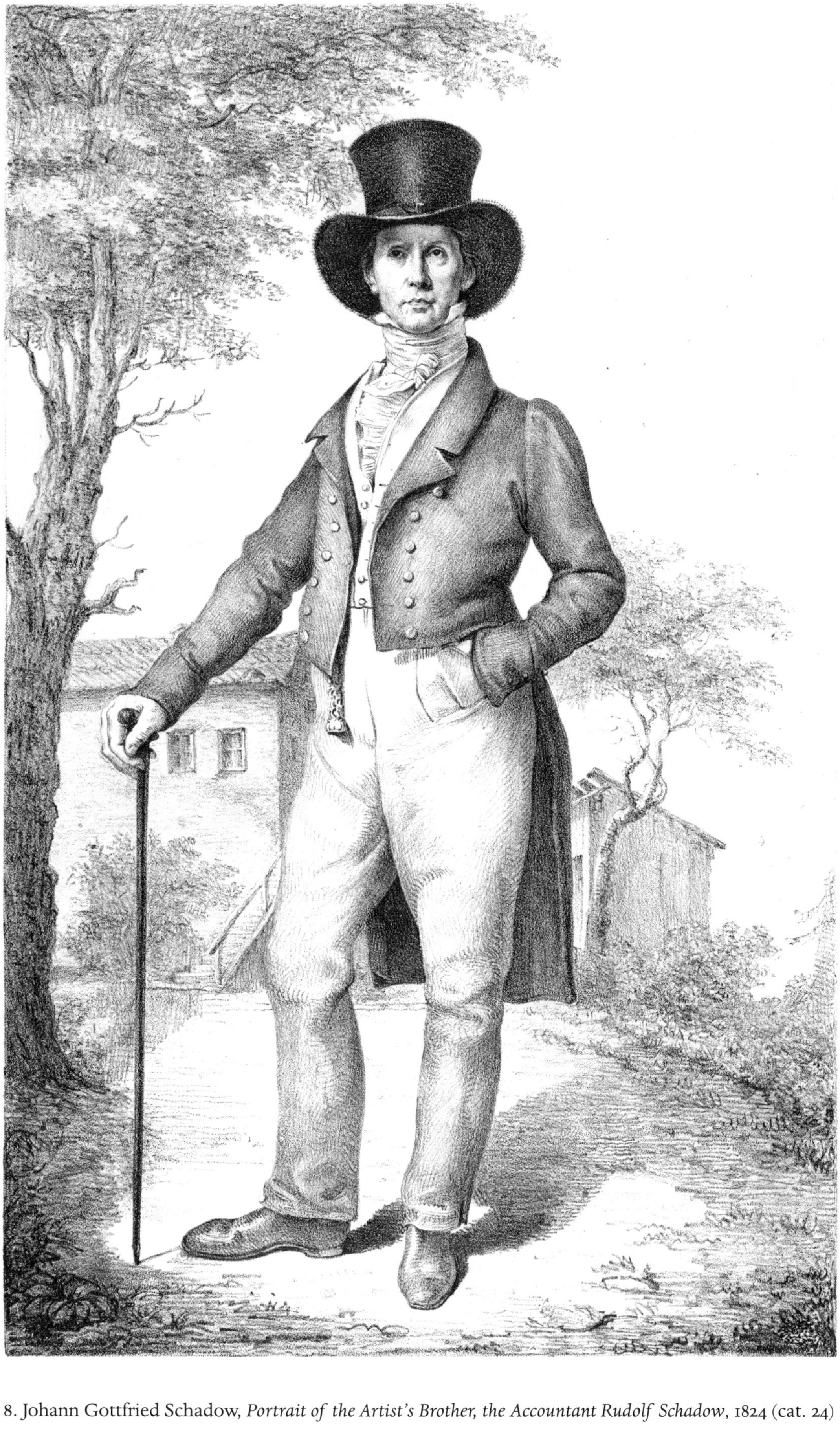

8. Johann Gottfried Schadow, *Portrait of the Artist's Brother, the Accountant Rudolf Schadow*, 1824 (cat. 24)

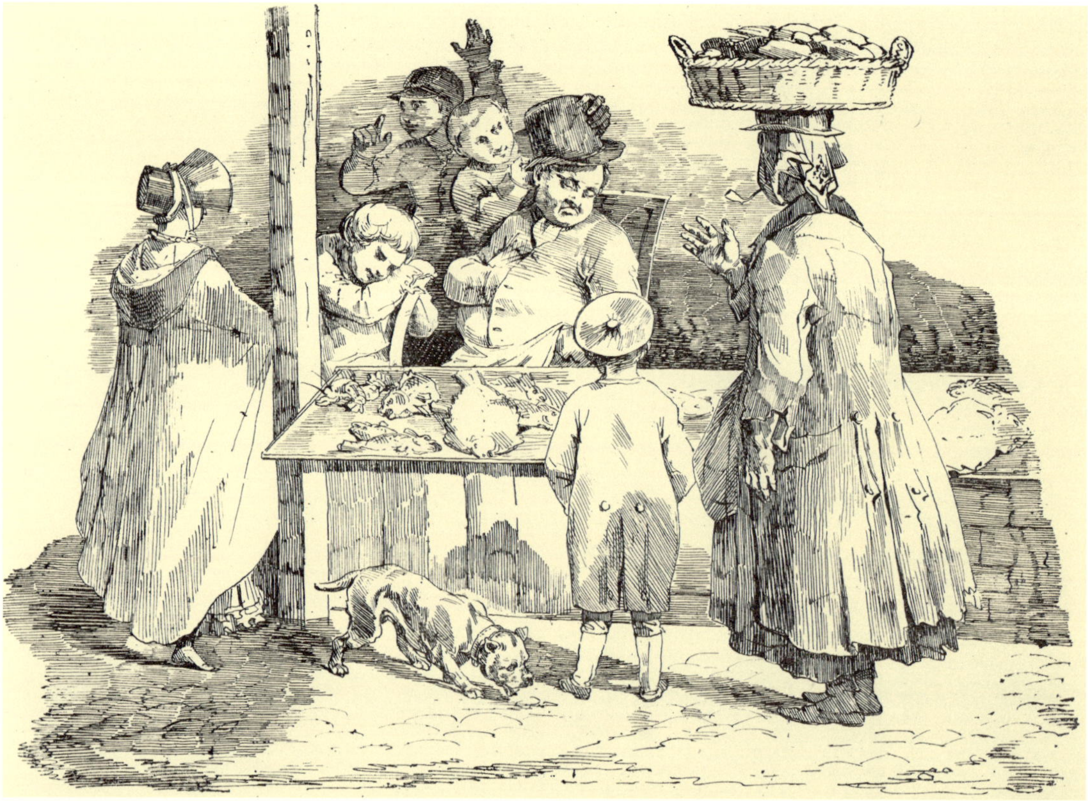

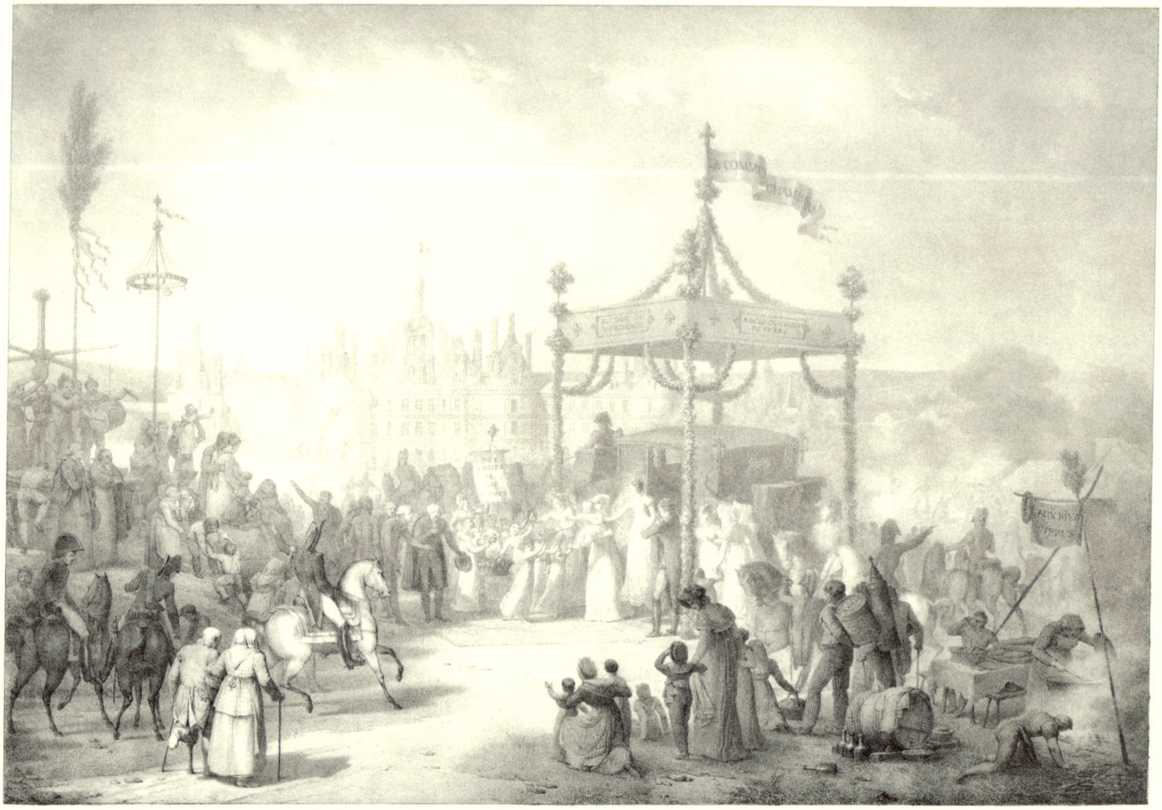

9. Théodore Géricault, *The Sleeping Fish Merchant*, 1820 (cat. 11)

10. Jean Baptiste Isabey, *Arrival of His Royal Highness, the Duke of Bordeaux, at Chambord*, 1821 (cat. 17)

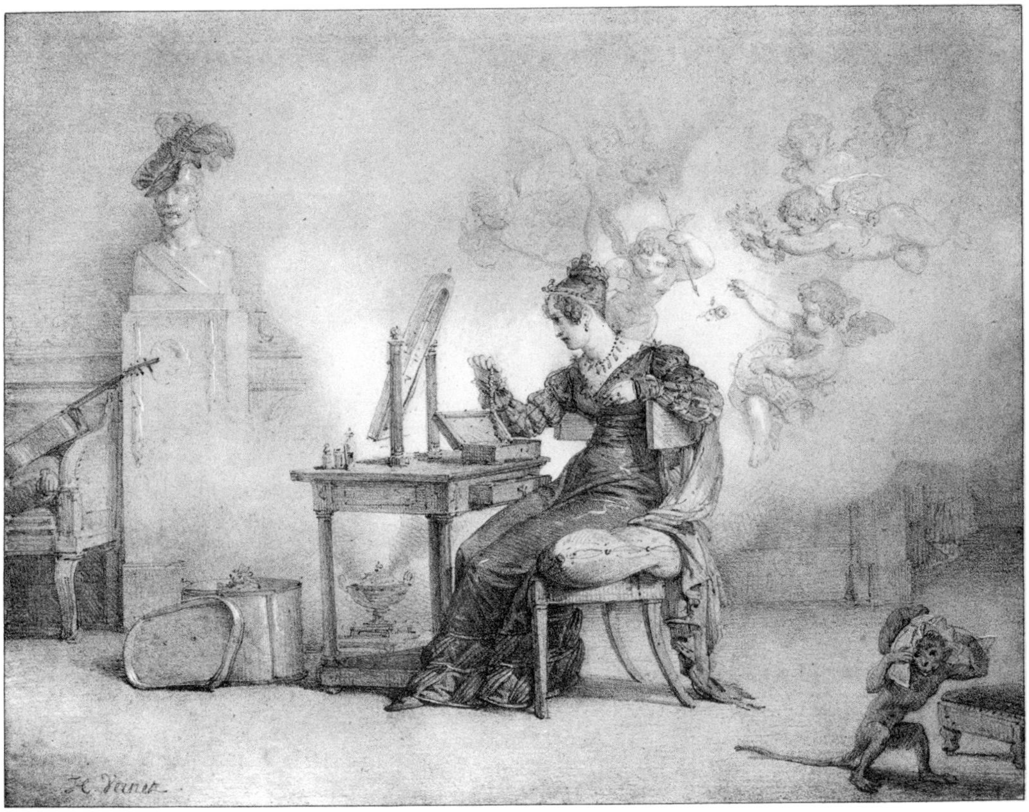

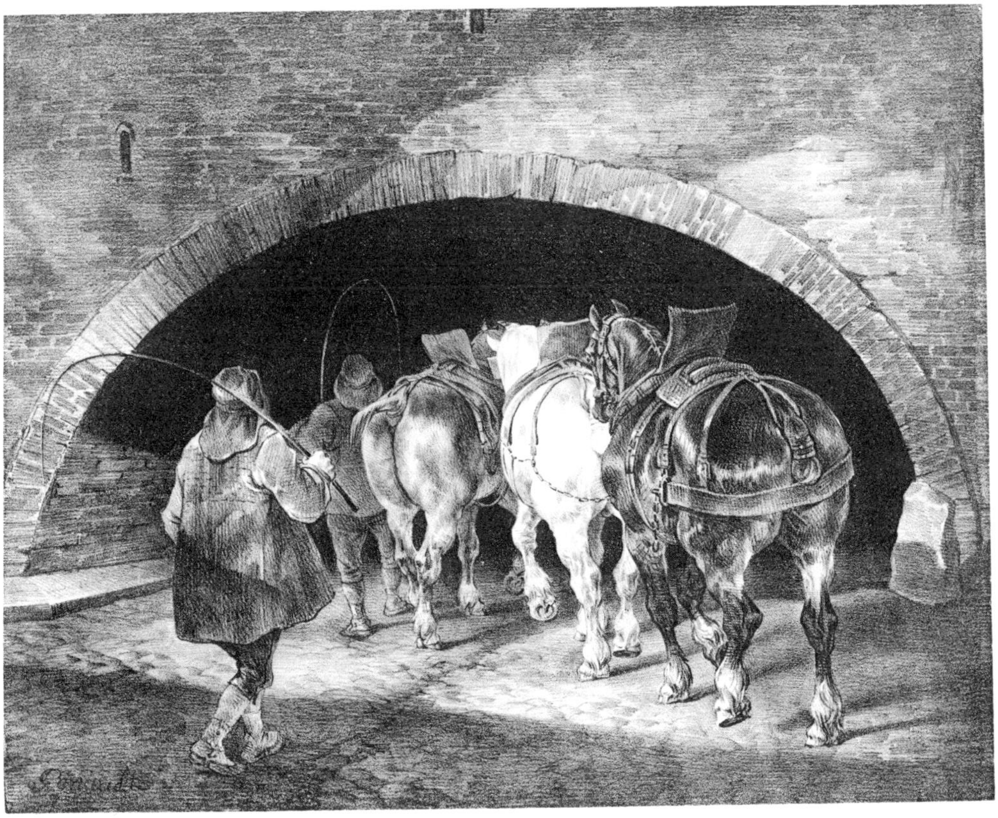

11. Horace Vernet, *The Young Widow* (from *Fables of La Fontaine*), 1818 (cat. 110)

12. Théodore Géricault, *Entrance to the Adelphi Wharf*, 1821 (cat. 12)

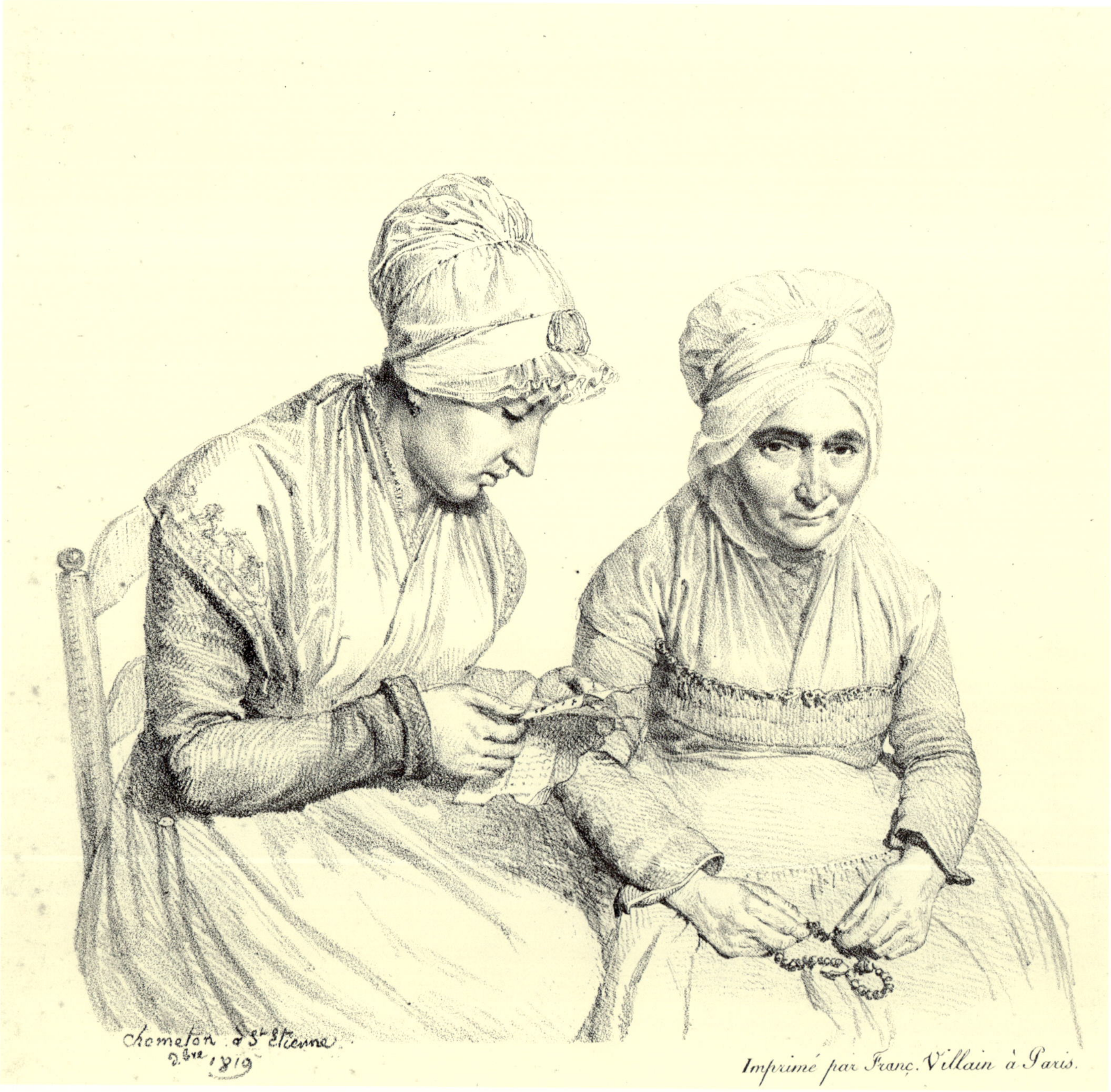

13. Jean Baptiste Chometon, *The Artist's Mother and Sister*, 1819 (cat. 20)

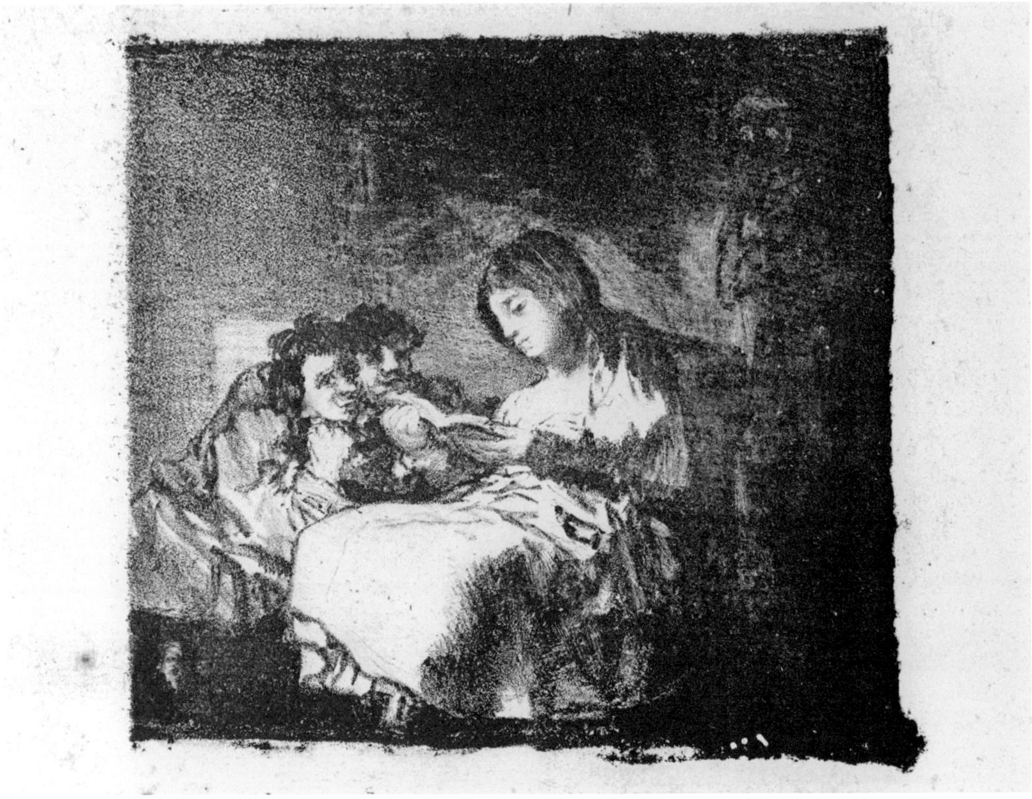

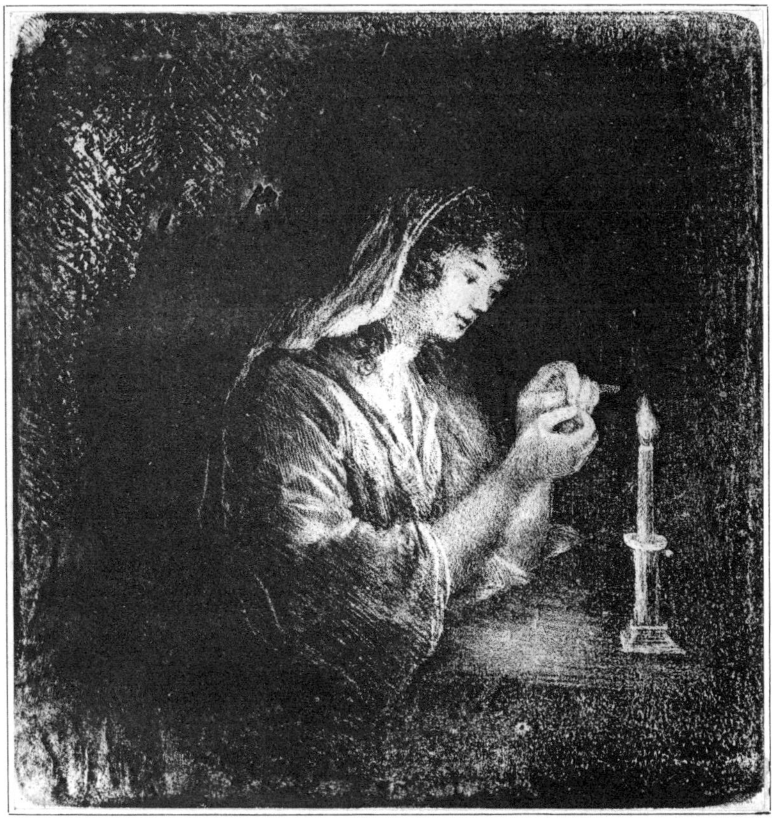

14. Francisco Goya, *Woman Reading to Two Children*, probably 1819-22 (cat. 95)

15. D.J. Redman, *Woman Threading a Needle by Candlelight*, about 1815 (cat. 99)

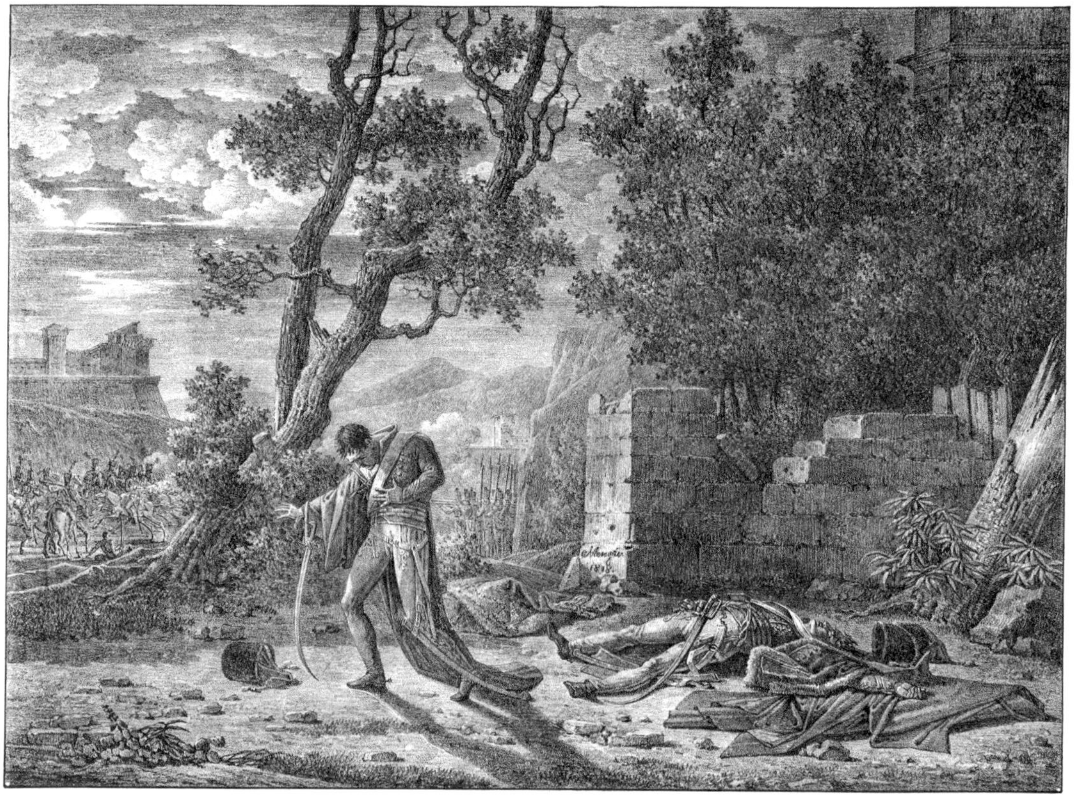

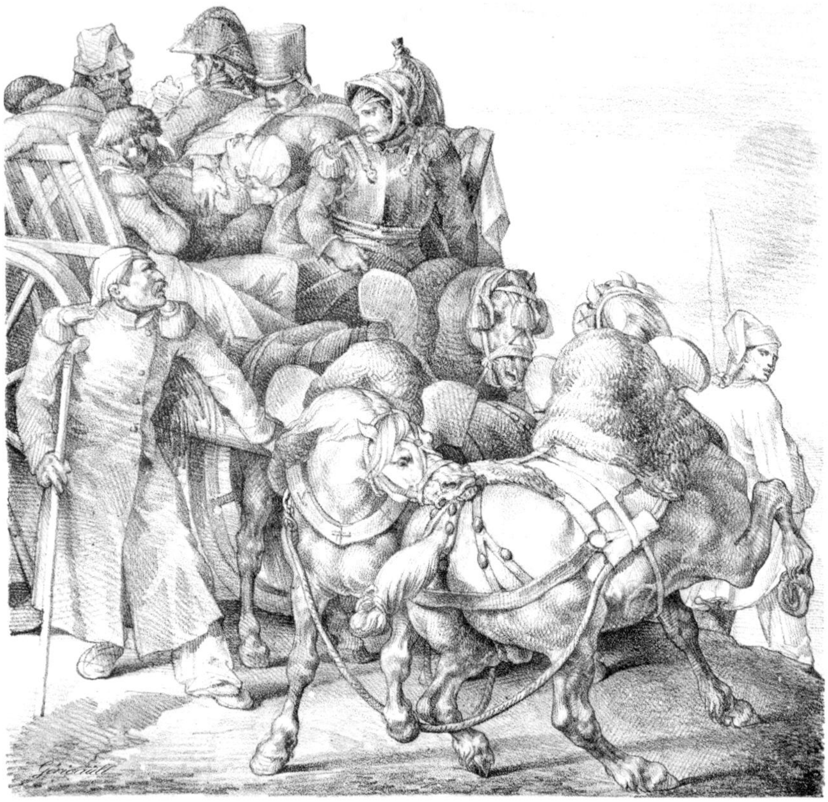

16. Antoine Pierre Mongin, *The Duel*, 1818 (cat. 86)

17. Théodore Géricault, *Wagon Loaded with Wounded Soldiers*, 1818 (cat. 83)

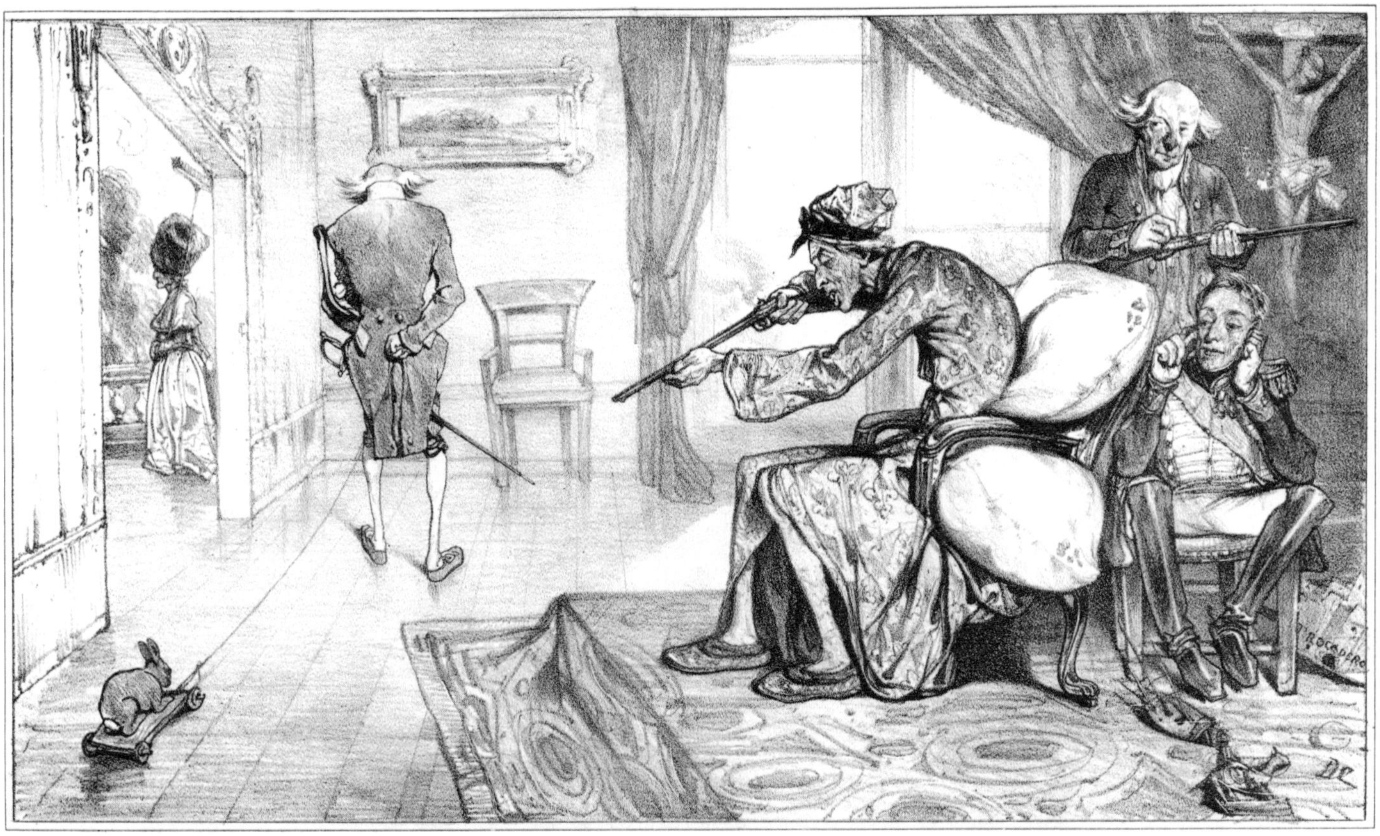

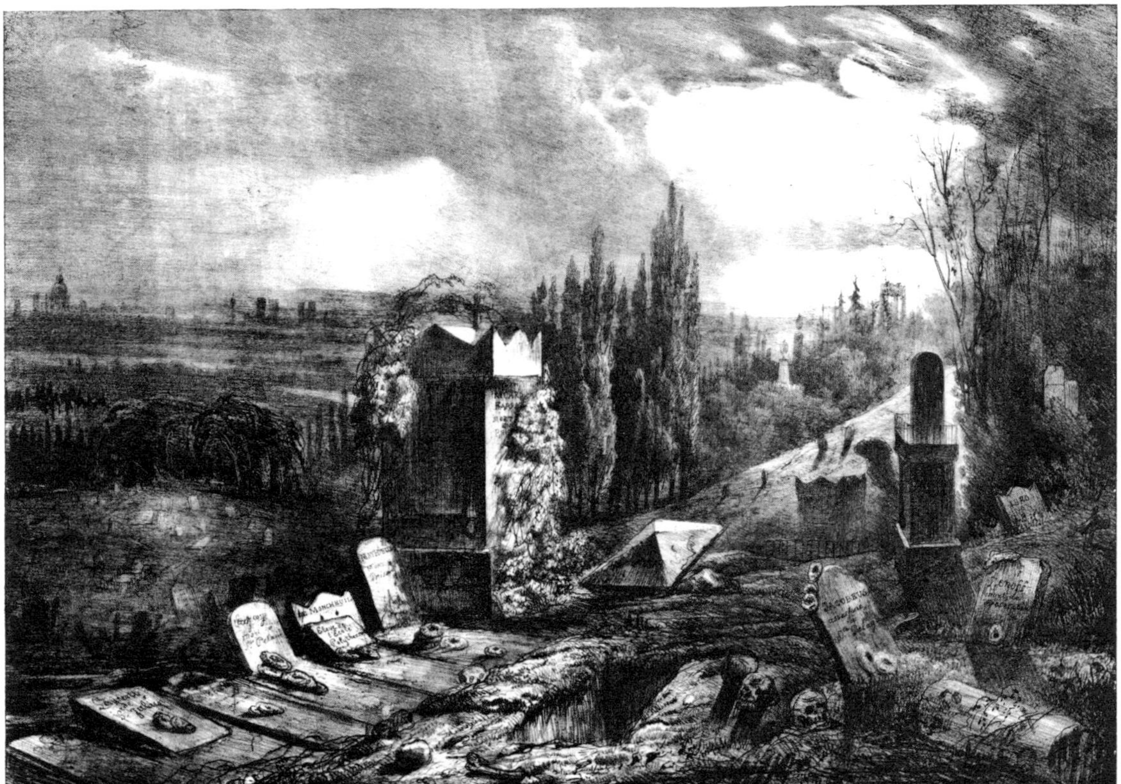

18. Alexandre Gabriel Decamps, *Year of Grace 1840, in the Glorious Reign of Charles X (extract from the court circular of the ex-king)*, 1830 (cat. 14)

19. Paul Huet, *Full and Total Amnesty Granted by Death in 1832* (cat. 13)

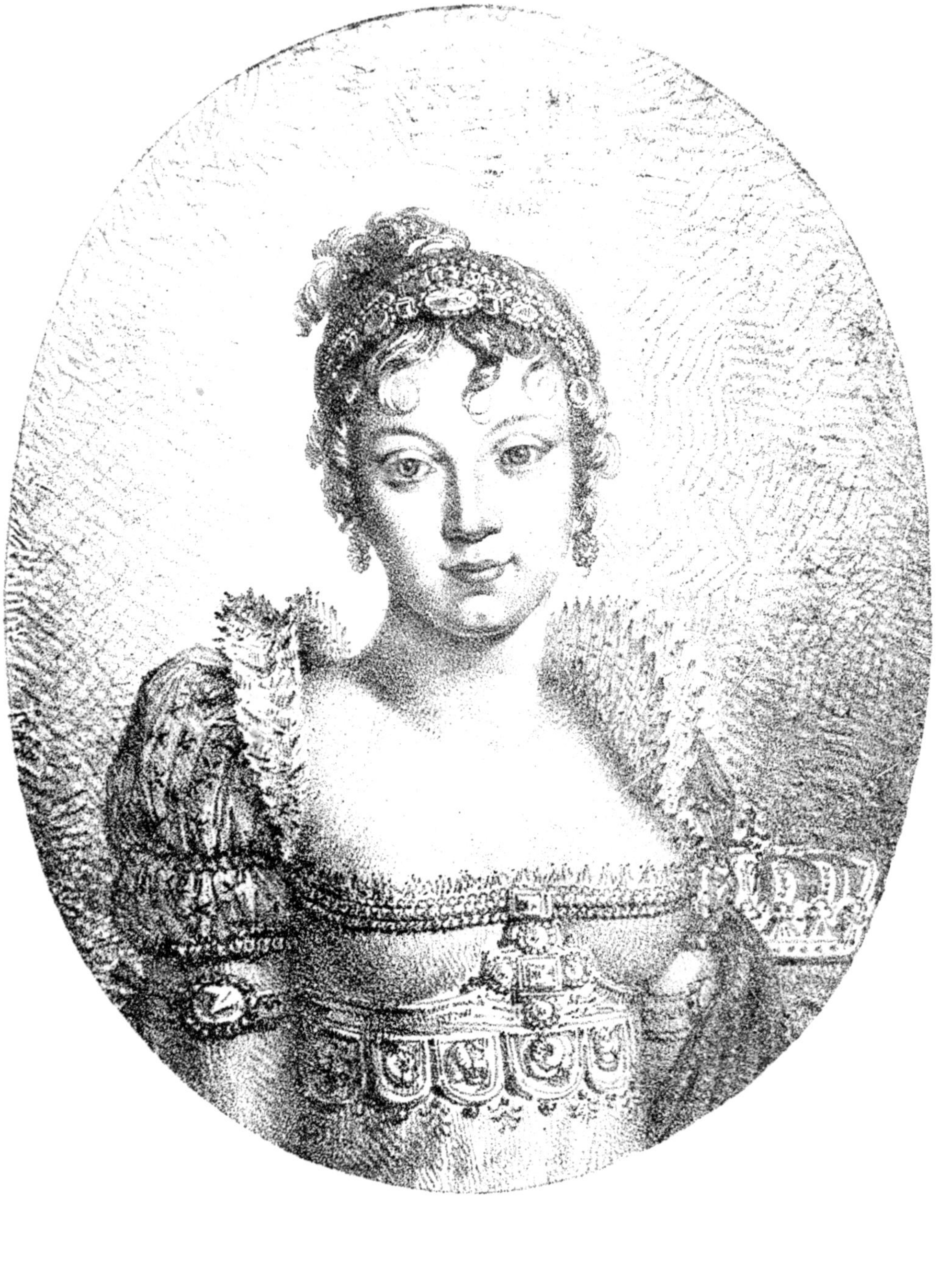

20. Anonymous, Italian (Milan), *The Empress Marie Louise*, 1811-12 (cat. 25)

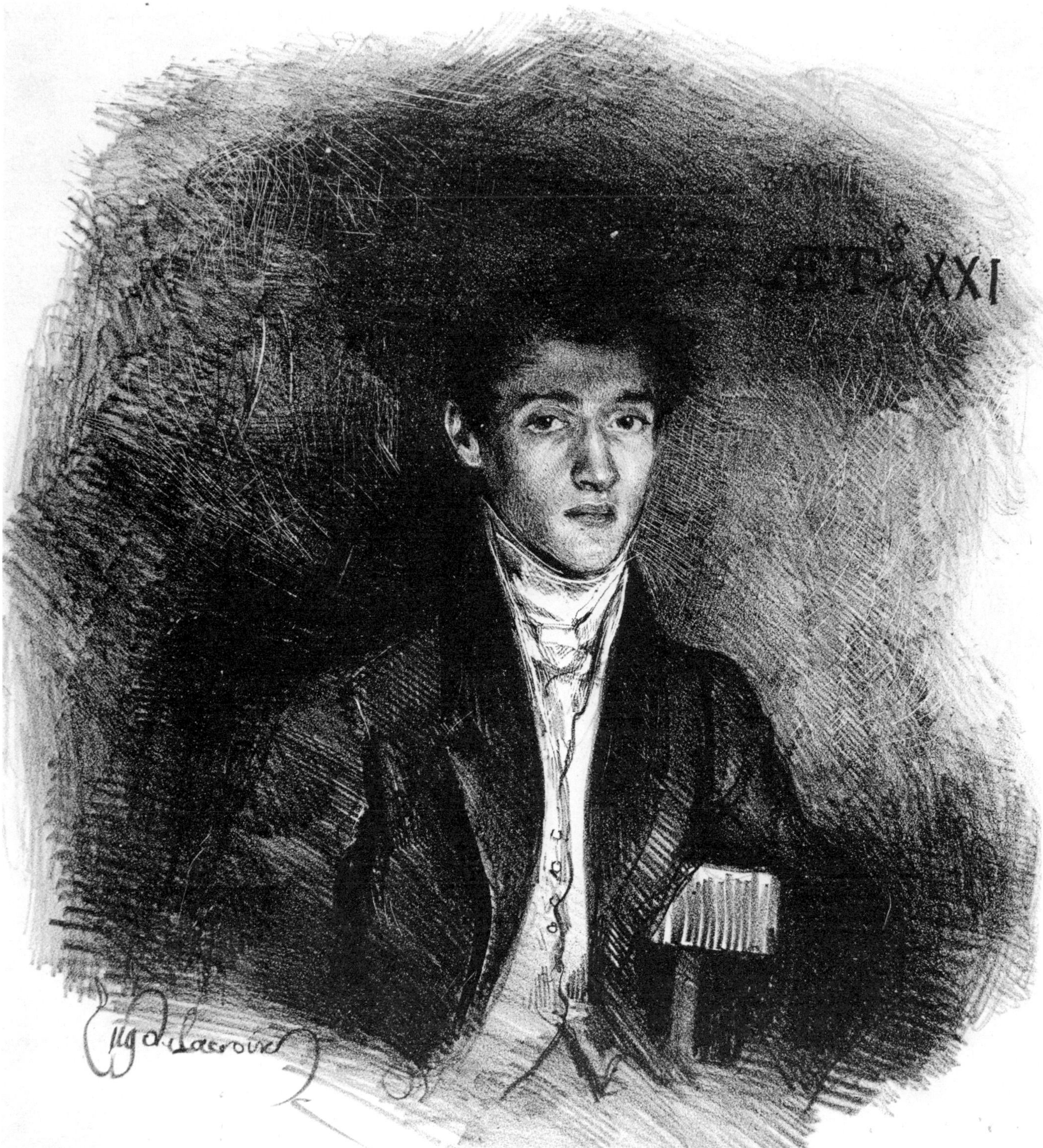

21. Eugène Delacroix, *Baron Schwiter*, 1826 (cat. 30)

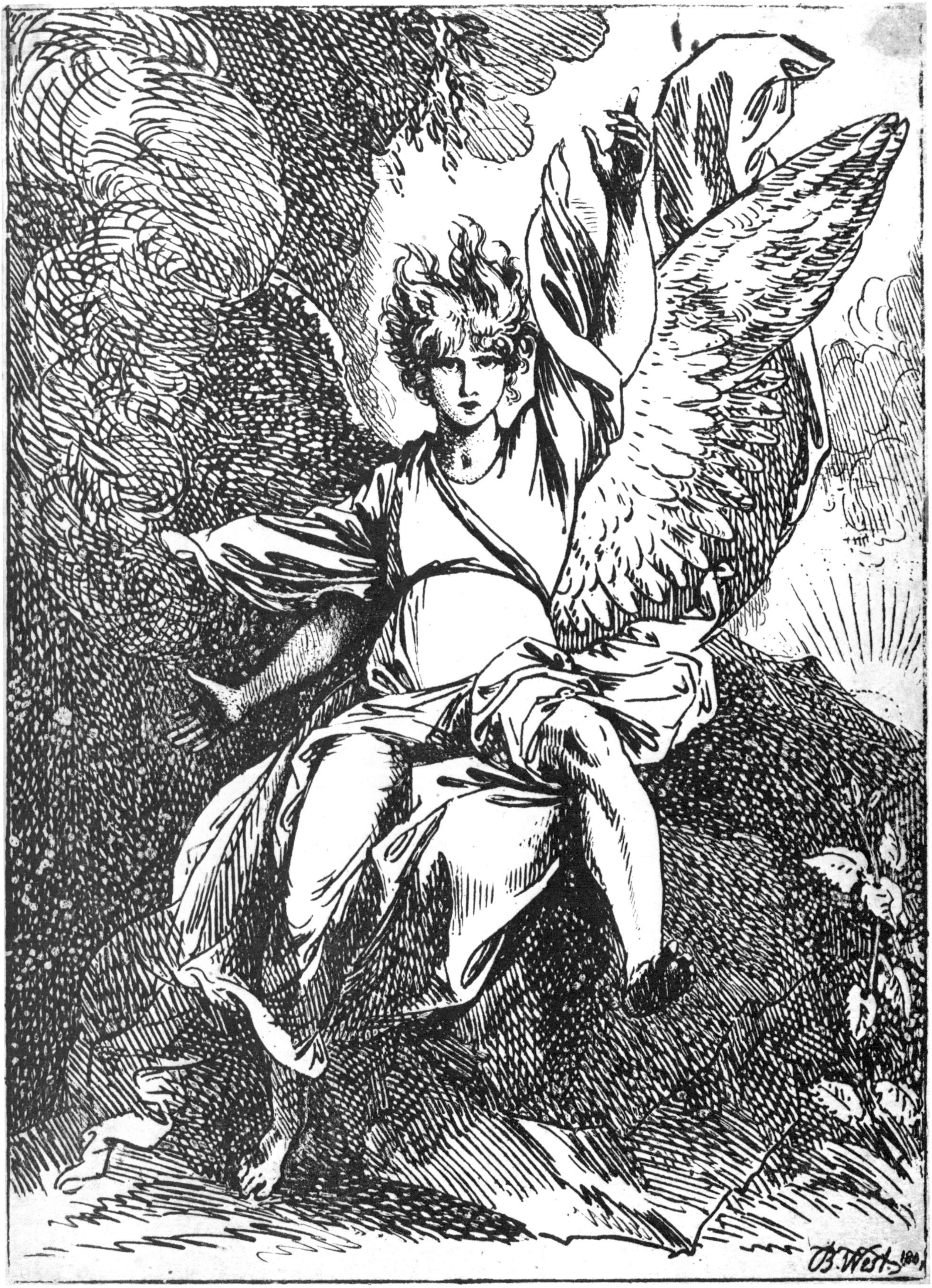

22. Benjamin West, *Angel of the Resurrection*, 1801 (cat. 48)

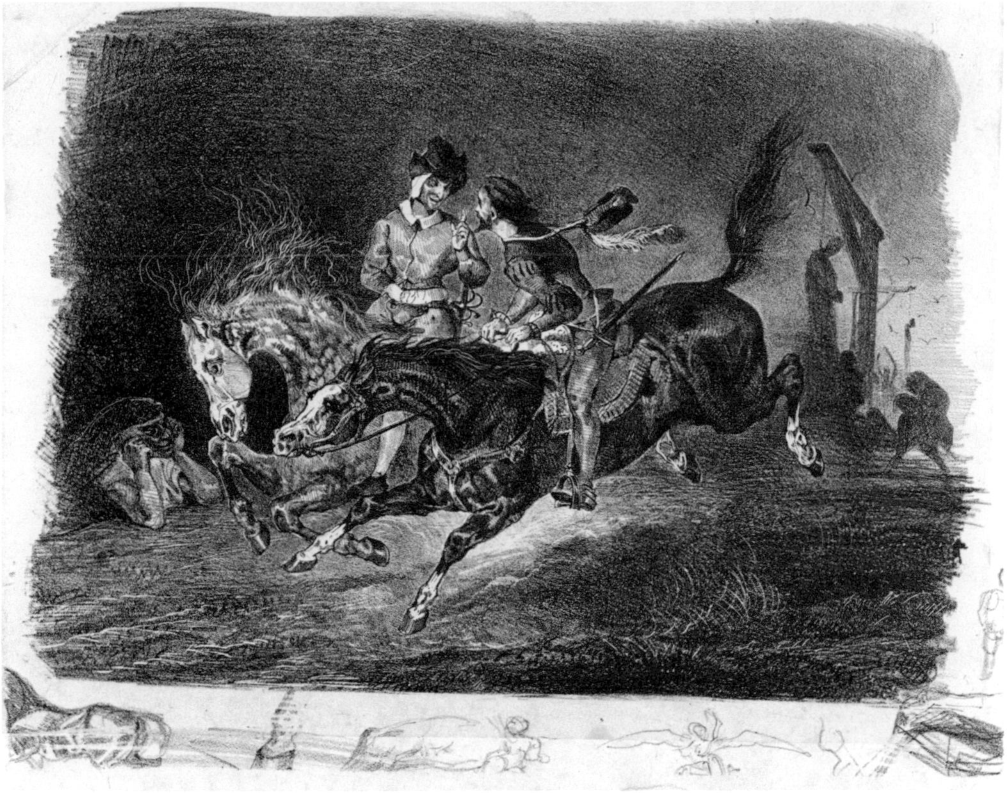

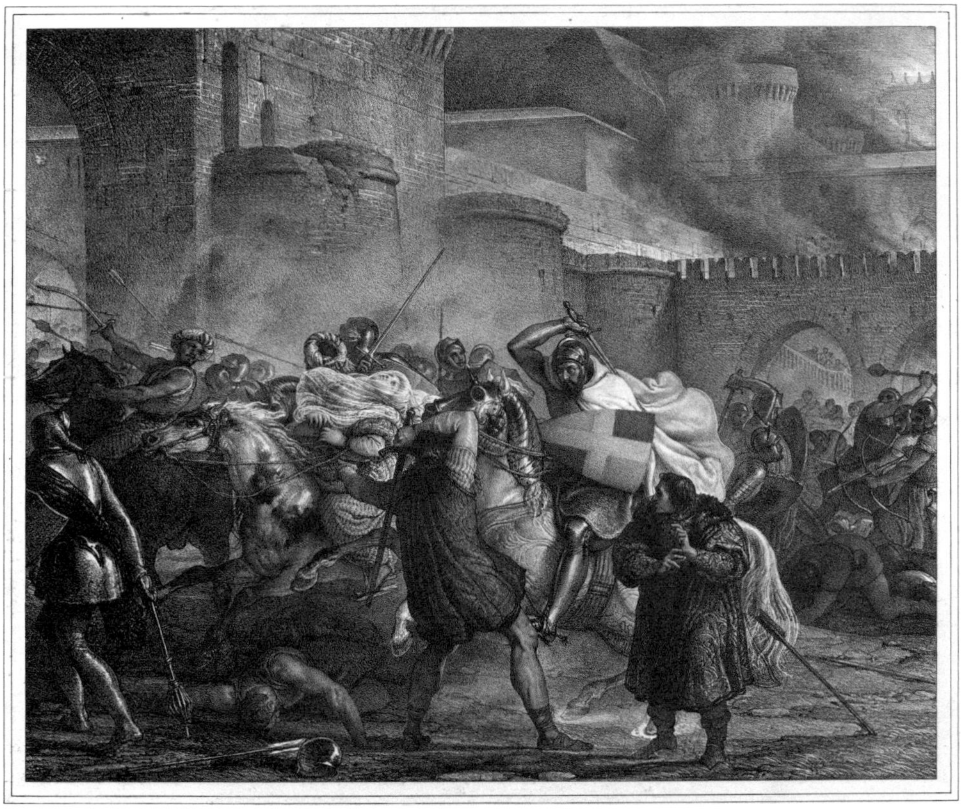

23. Eugène Delacroix, *Faust and Mephistopheles galloping on the Night of the Witches' Sabbath*, 1826-27 (cat. 34)

24. Francesco Hayez, *"Turn, false-hearted Templar"* (scene from *Ivanhoe)*, 1834 (cat. 32)

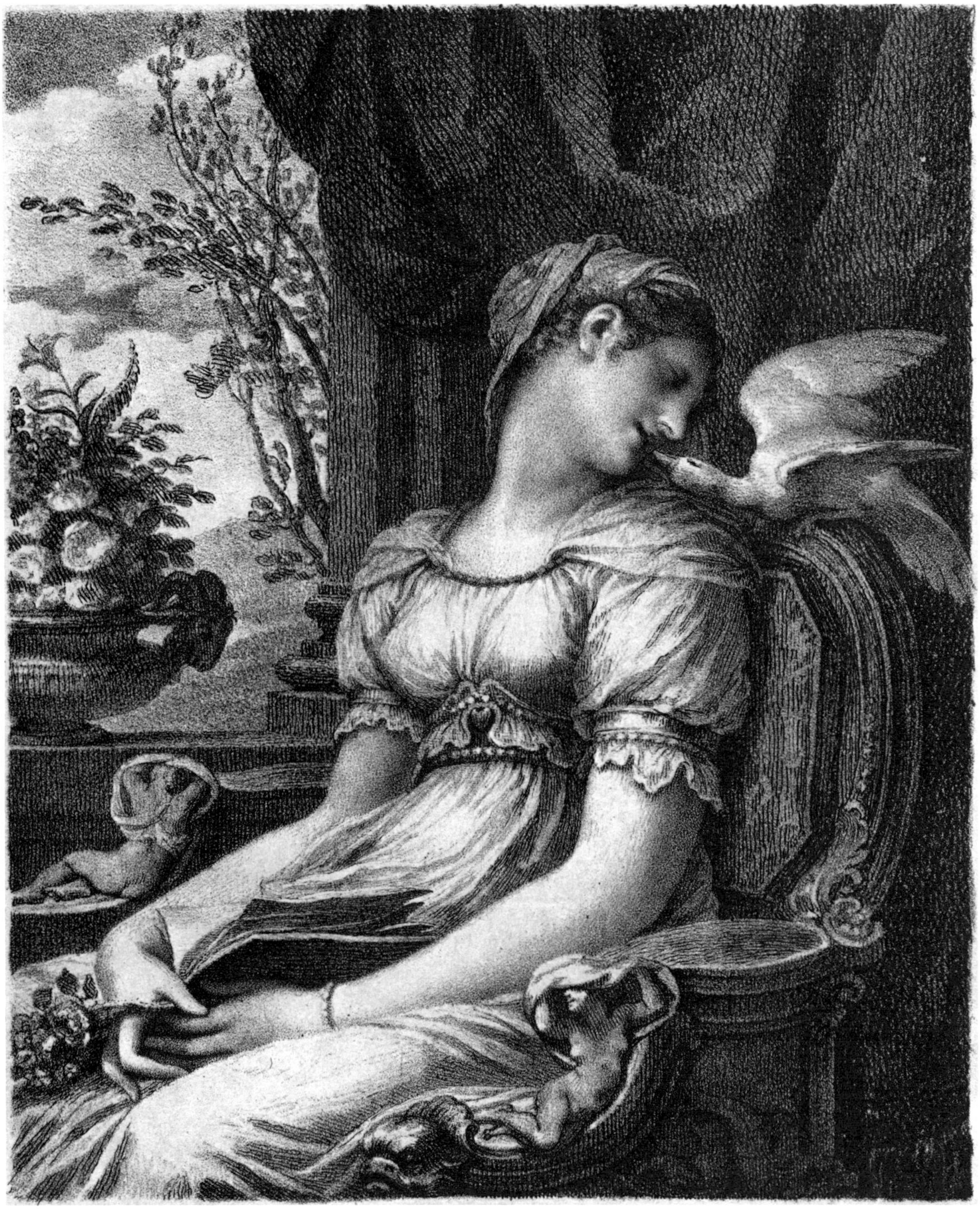

25. Pierre Paul Prud'hon, *Reading*, 1822 (cat. 42)

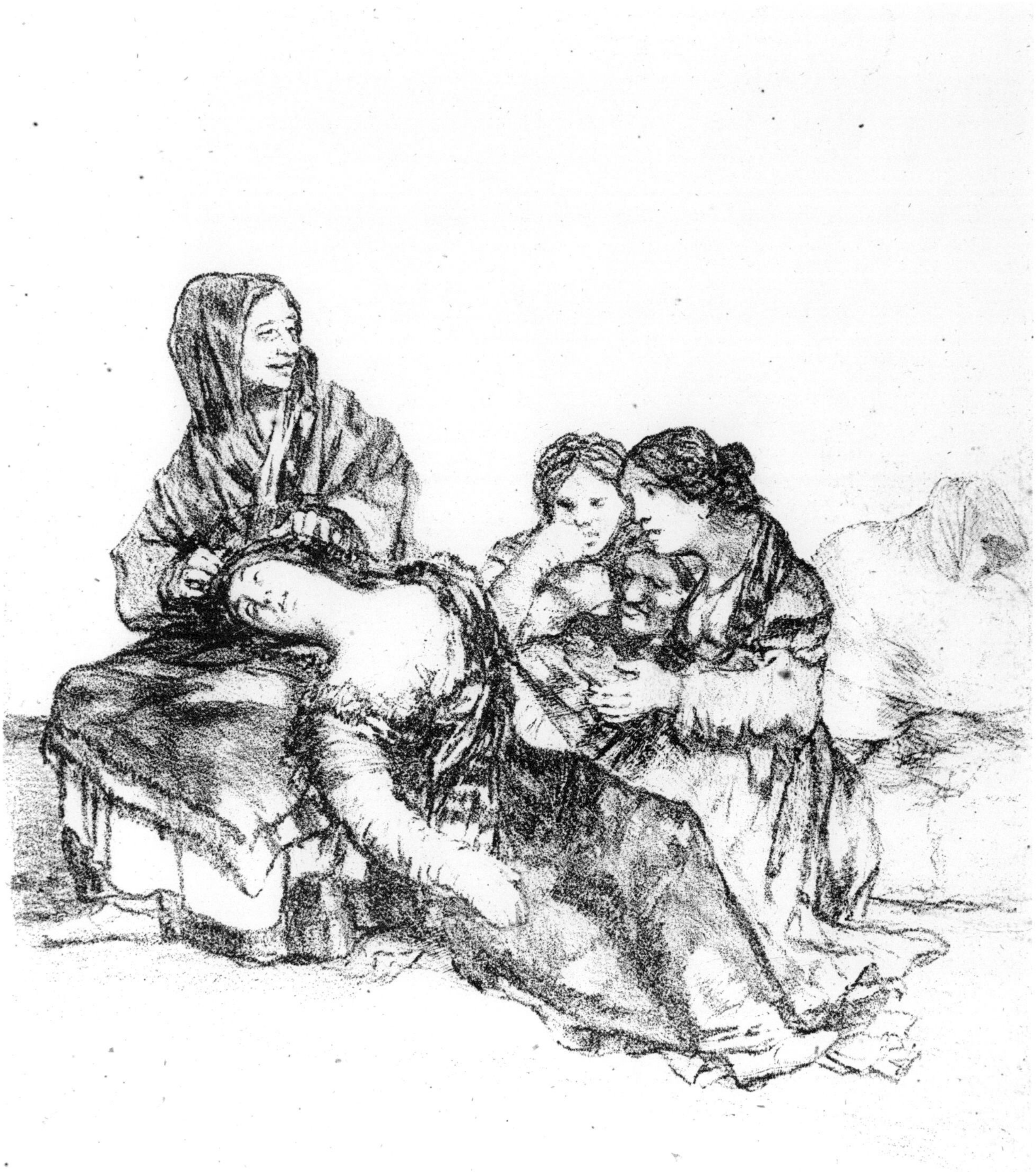

26. Francisco Goya, *Woman Asleep or in a Trance*, probably 1819-22 (cat. 37)

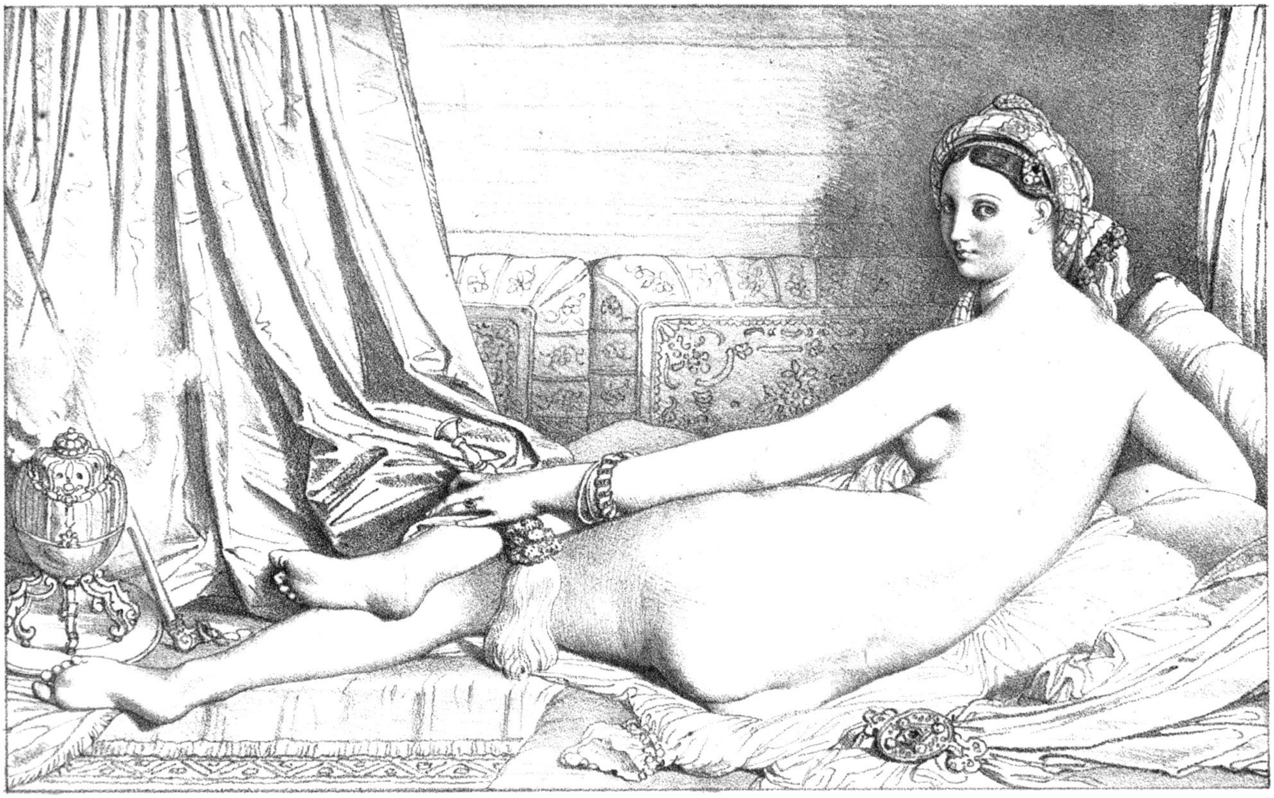

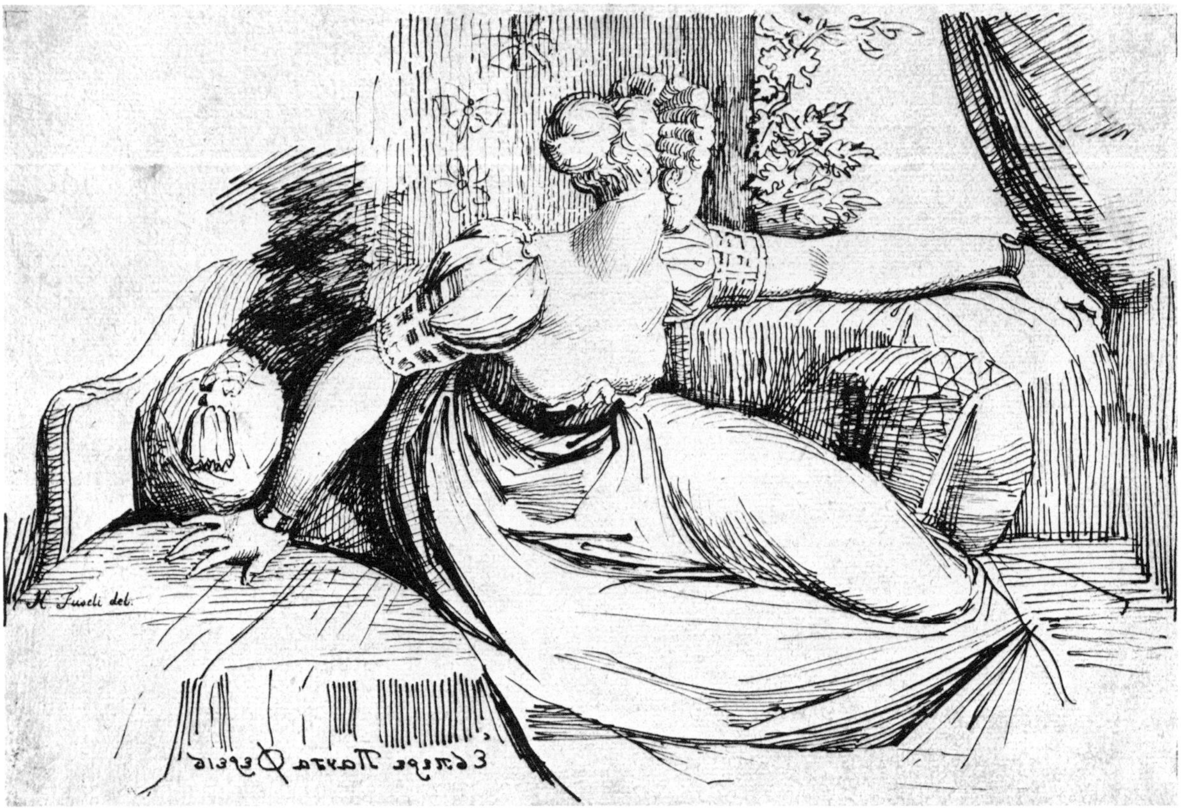

27. Jean Auguste Dominique Ingres, *Odalisque*, 1825 (cat. 38)

28. Henry Fuseli, *"Evening thou bringest all,"* 1802 (cat. 40)

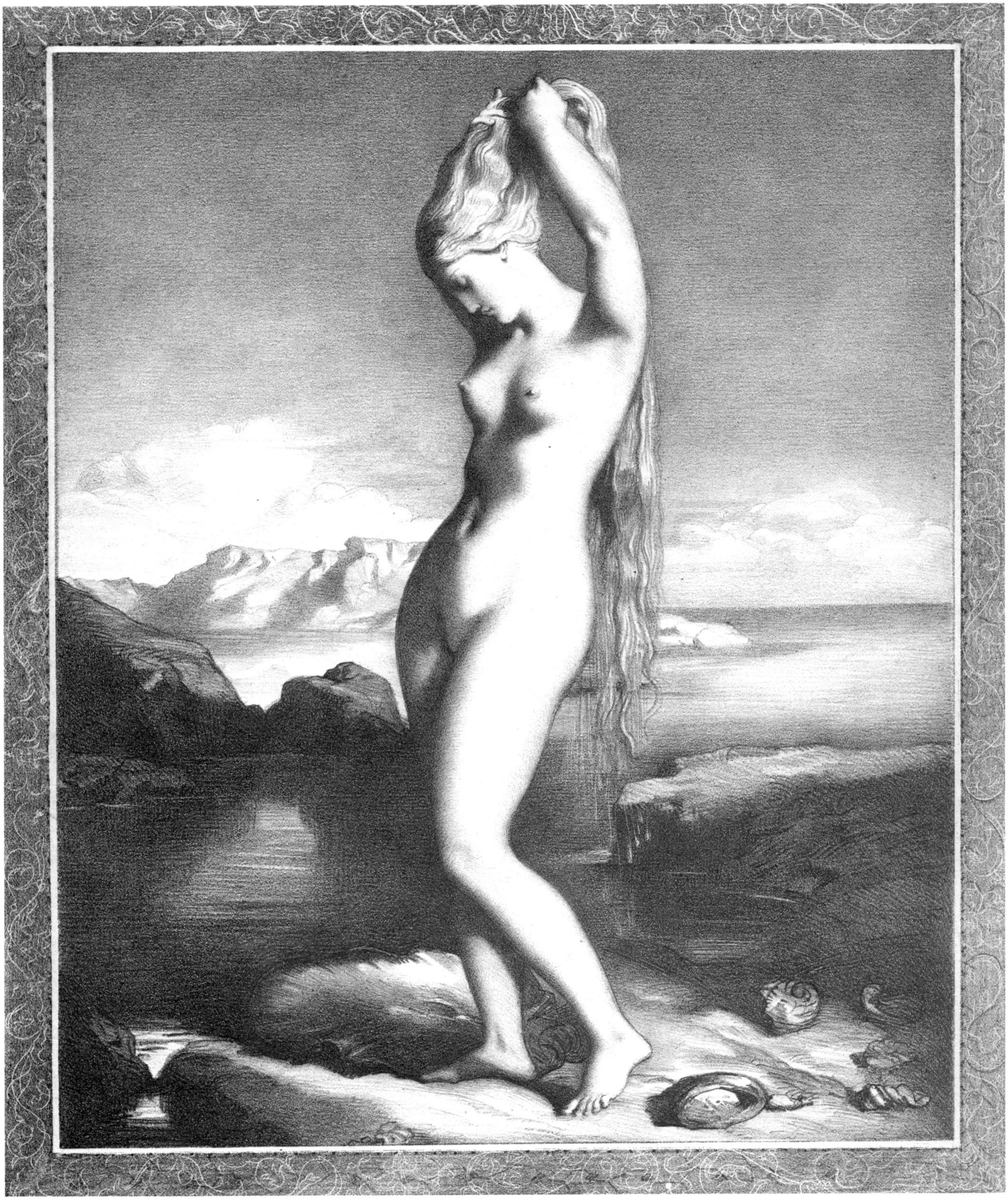

29. Théodore Chassériau, *Venus Rising from the Sea*, 1839 (cat. 43)

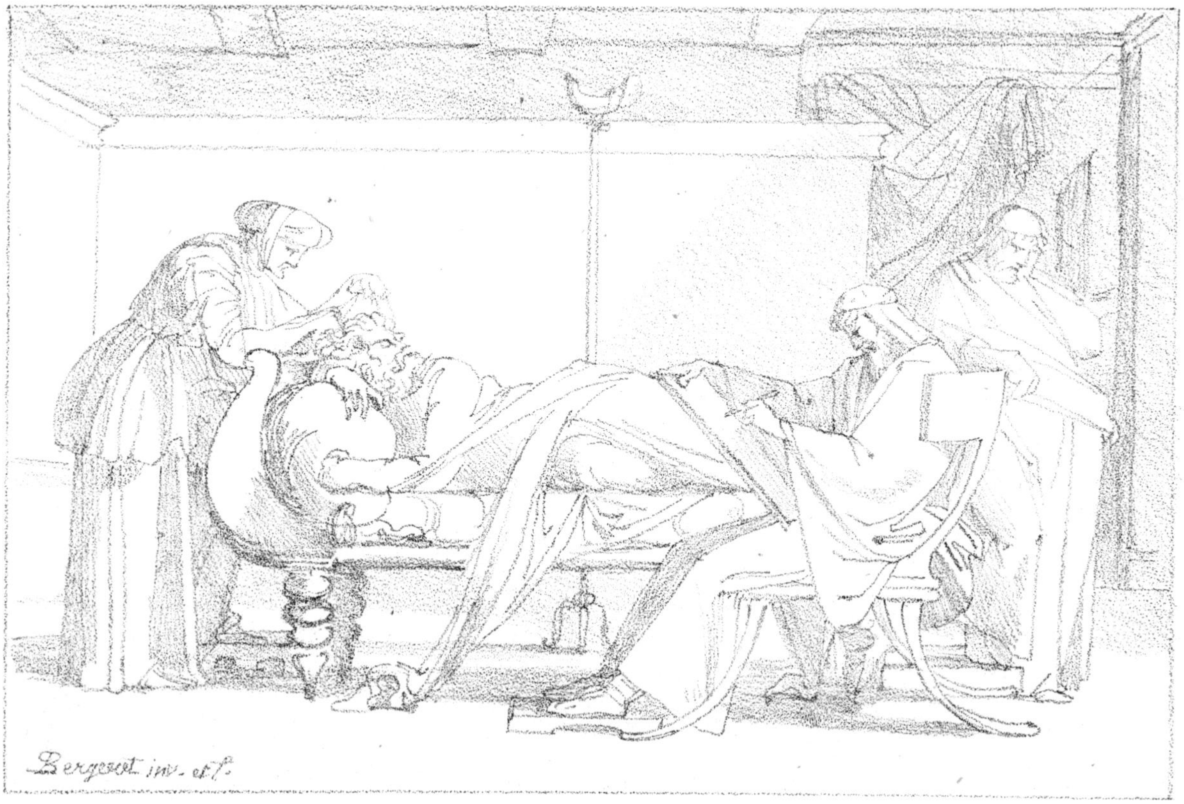

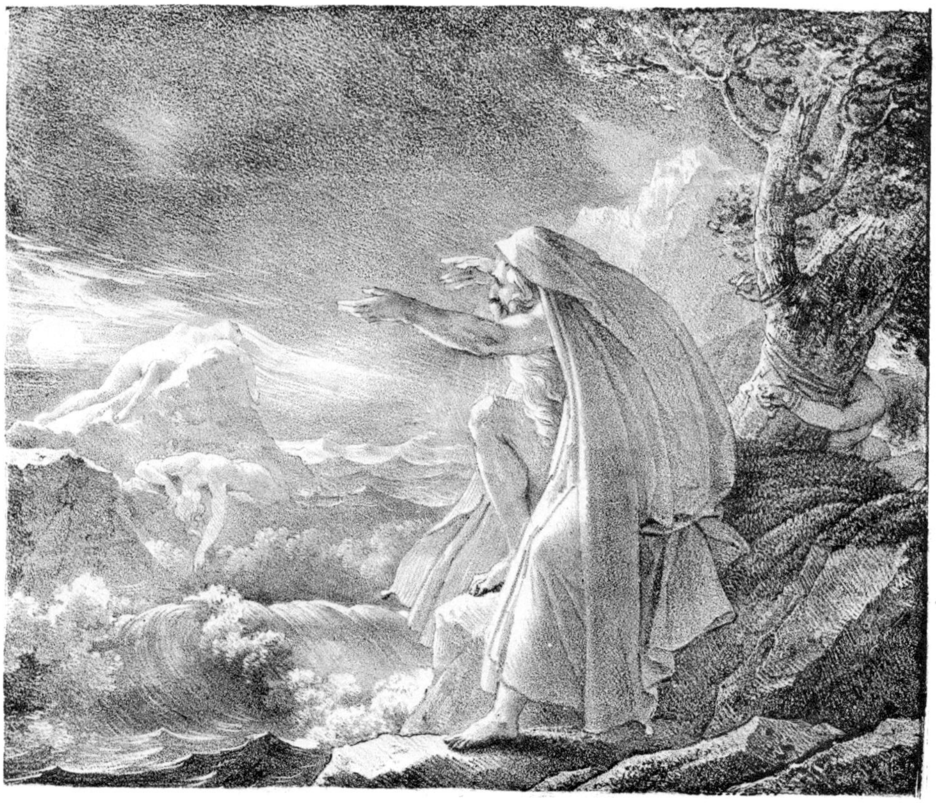

30. Pierre Nolasque Bergeret, *Deathbed Scene in Antiquity*, about 1804-05 (cat. 45)

31. Anne Louis Girodet-Trioson, *The Bard Armin Lamenting the Death of his Children*, about 1816 (cat. 44)

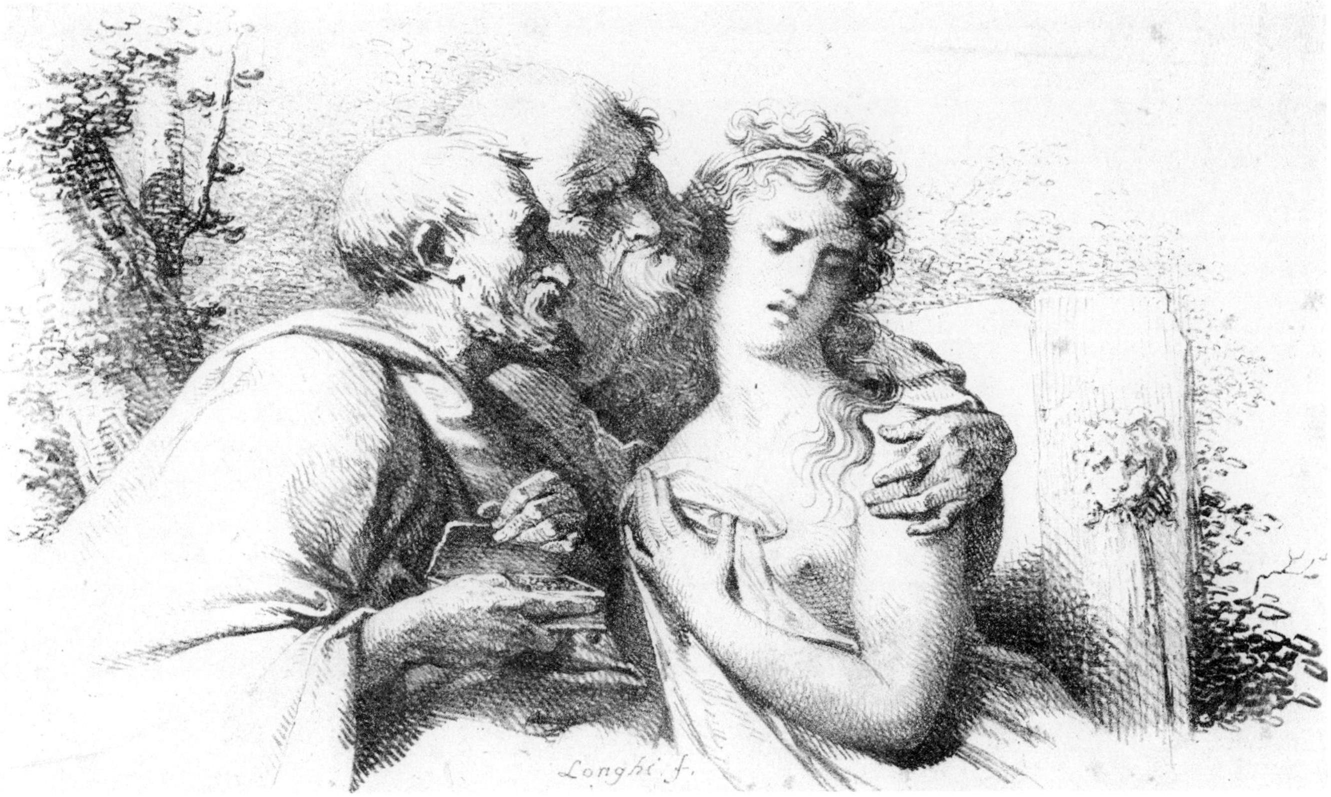

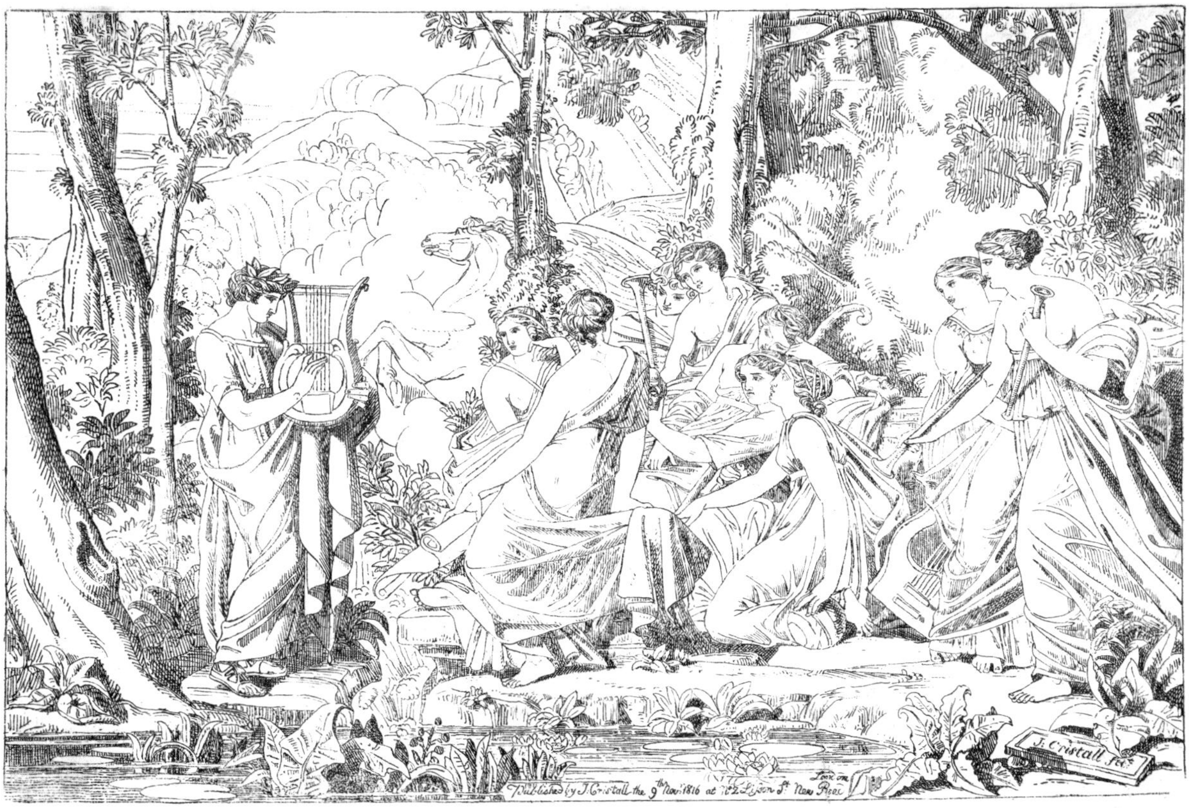

32. Giuseppe Longhi, *Susanna and the Elders*, 1821 (cat. 39)

33. Joshua Cristall, *Apollo and the Muses*, 1816 (cat. 47)

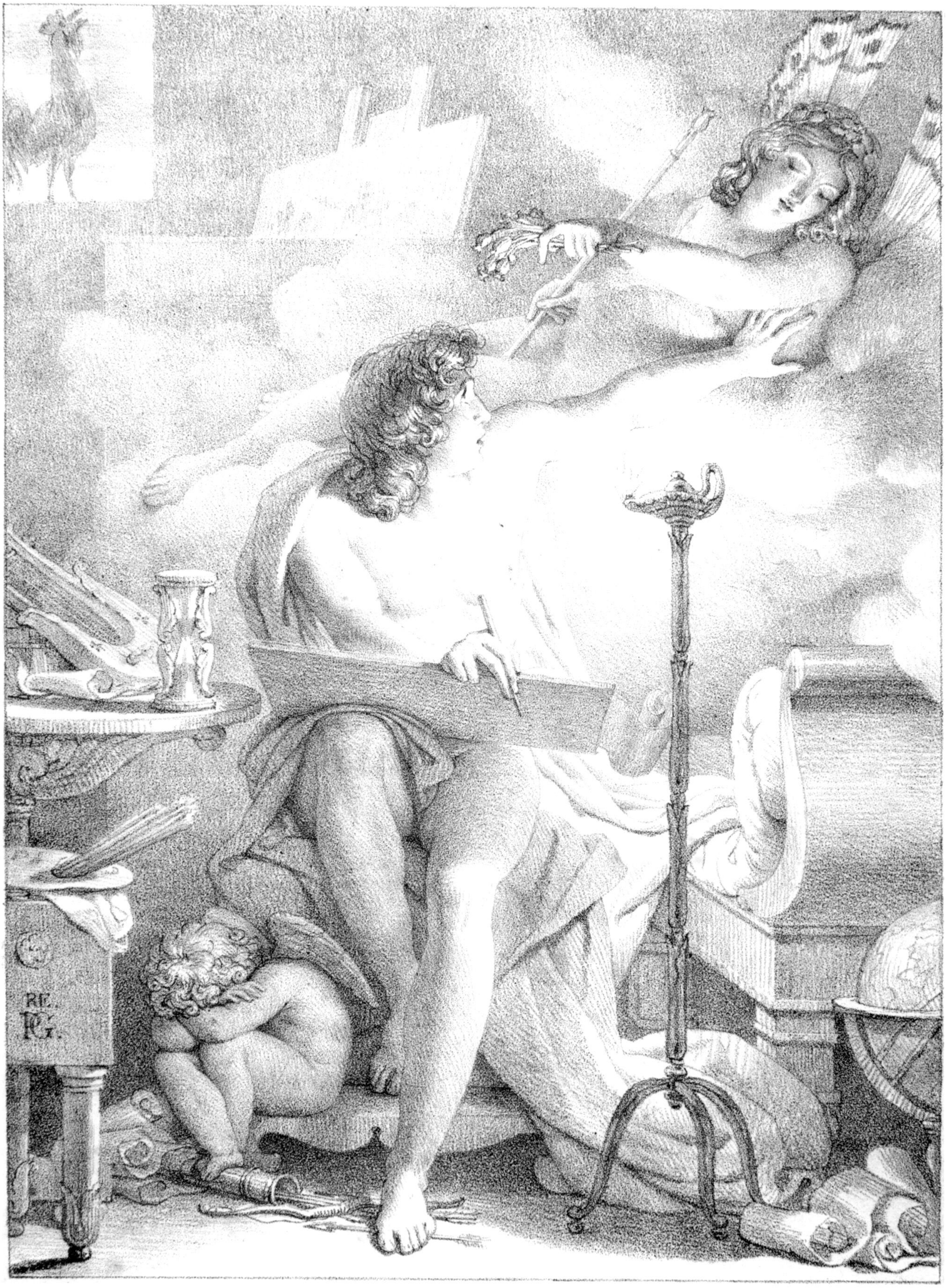

34. Pierre Narcisse Guérin, *The Vigilant One*, 1816 (cat. 101)

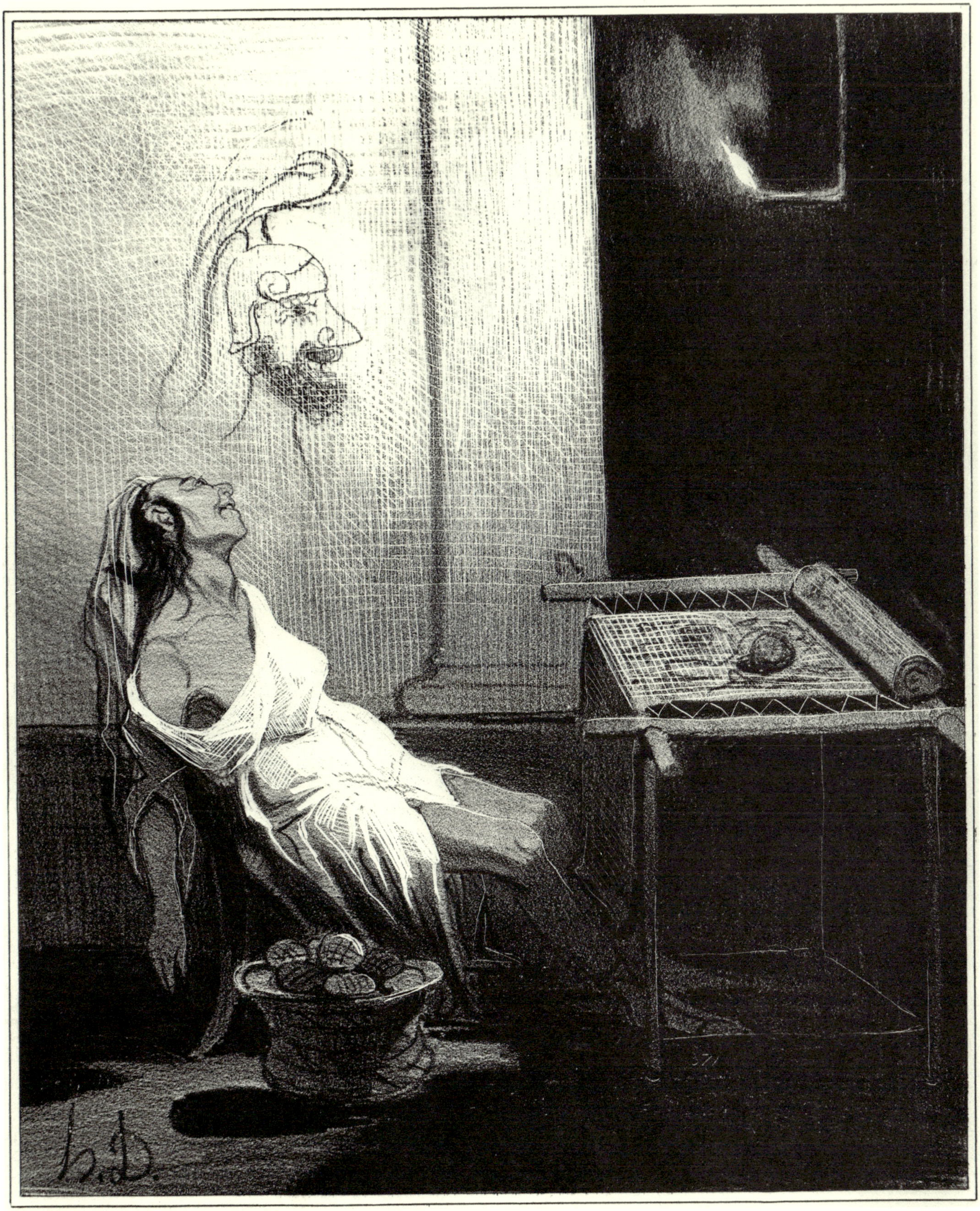

35. Honoré Daumier, *Penelope's Nights*, 1842 (cat. 100)

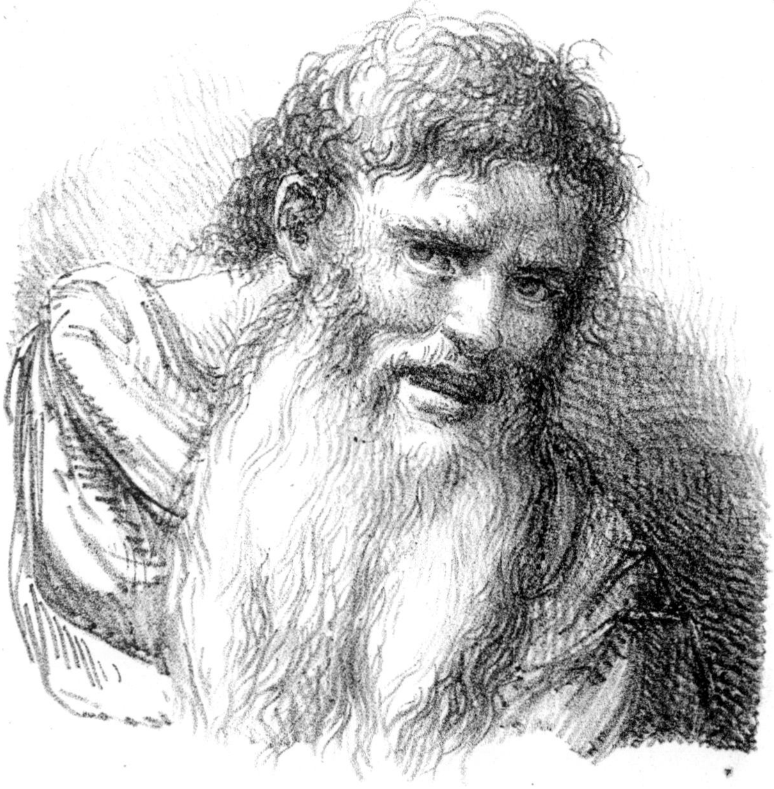

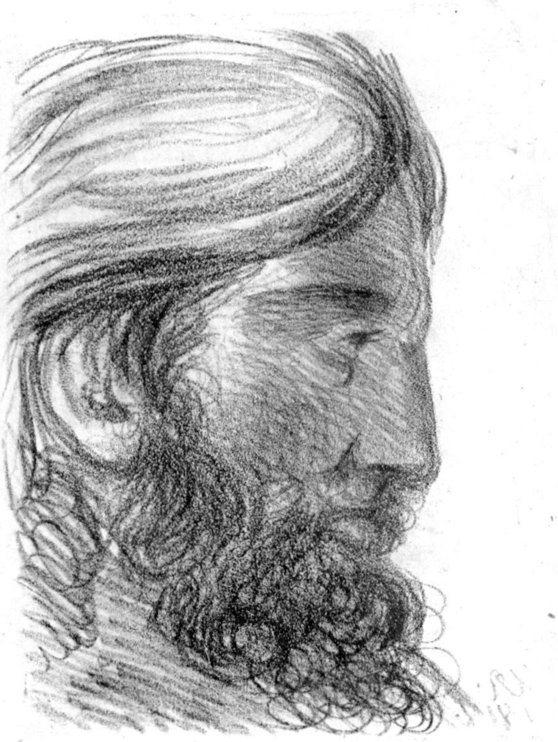

36. Andrea Appiani, *Head of a Bearded Man*, 1808-12 (cat. 106)

37. Wilhelm Reuter, *Head of a Bearded Man in Profile*, 1818 (cat. 103)

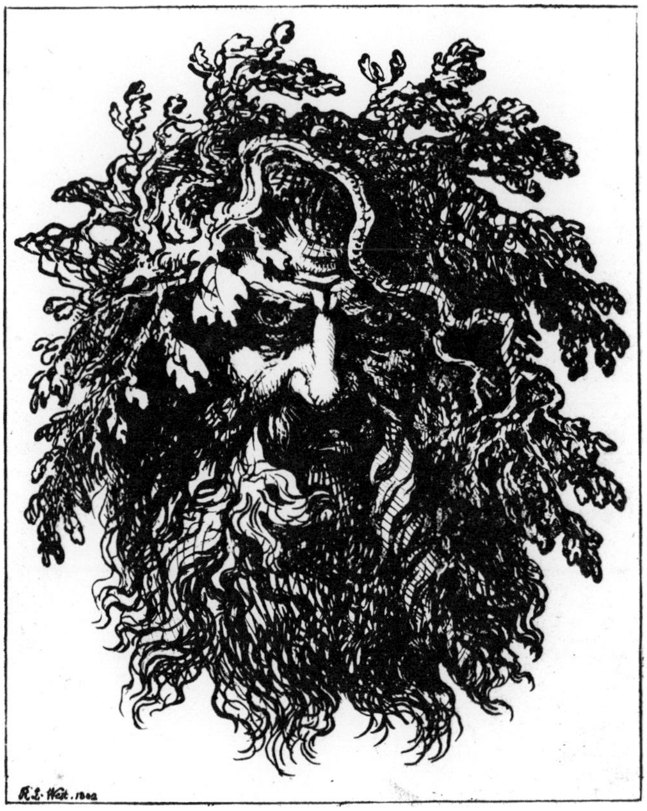

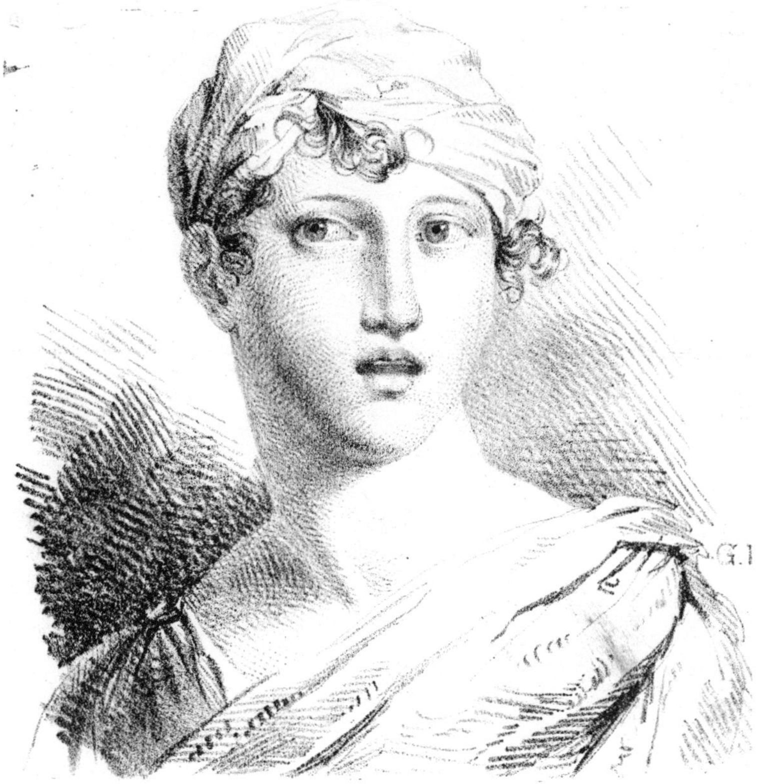

38. Raphael Lamar West, *Head of a Bearded Man Wreathed with Oak Branches*, 1802 (cat. 74)

39. Giuseppe Longhi, *Head of a Young Woman Wearing a Turban*, 1808-12 (cat. 102)

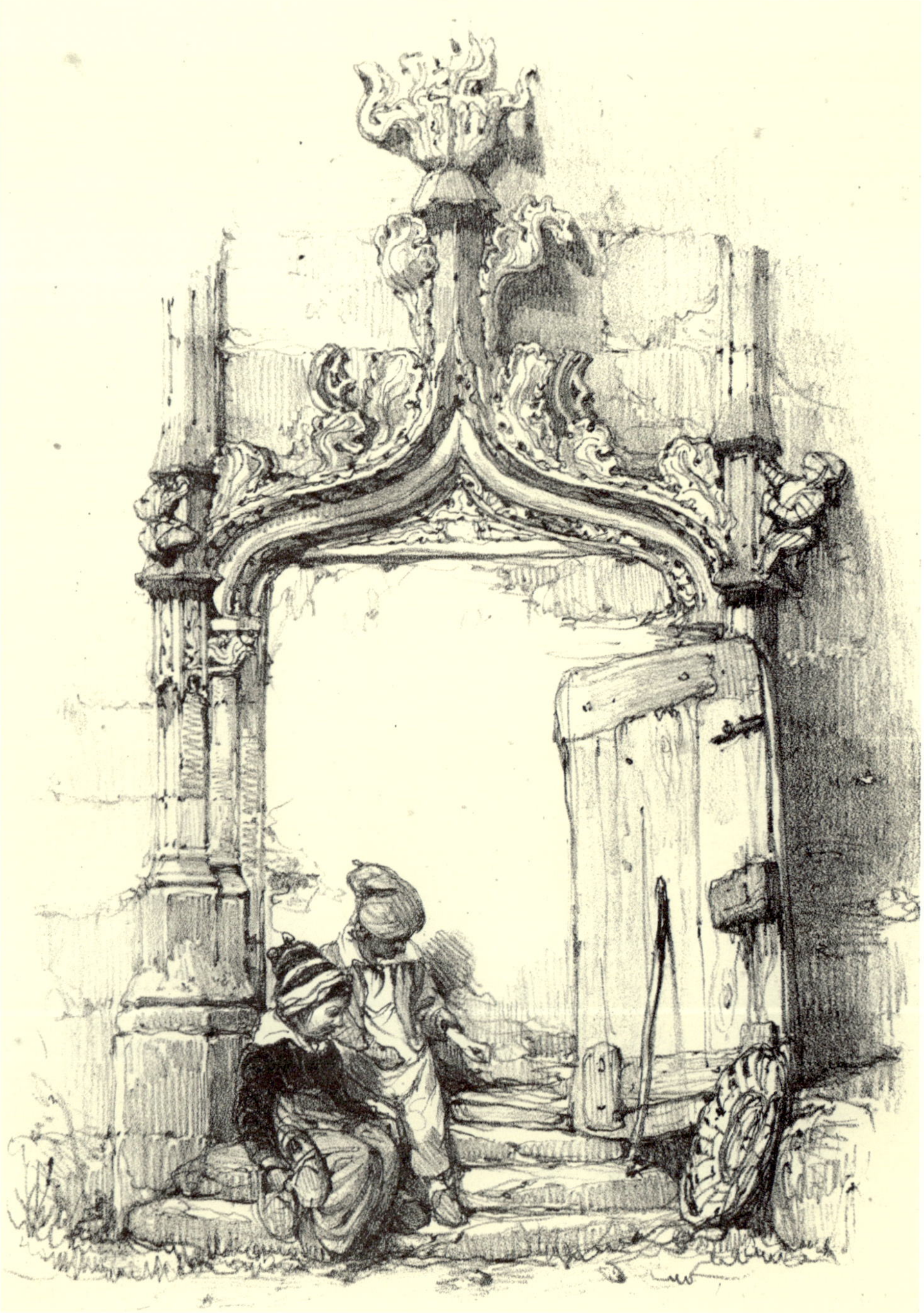

40. Richard Parkes Bonington, *Remains of a Gothic Doorway*, 1824 (cat. 57)

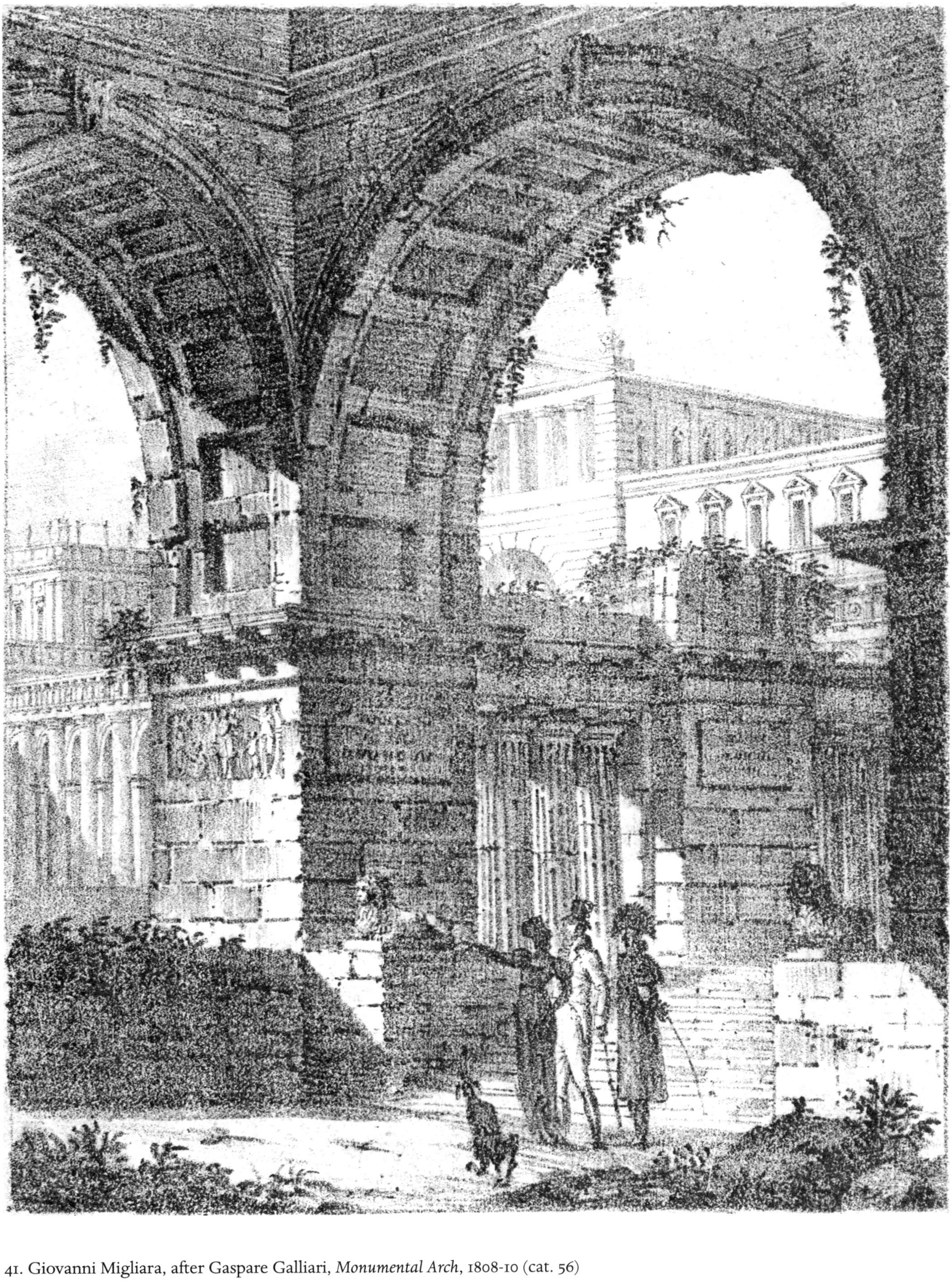

41. Giovanni Migliara, after Gaspare Galliari, *Monumental Arch*, 1808-10 (cat. 56)

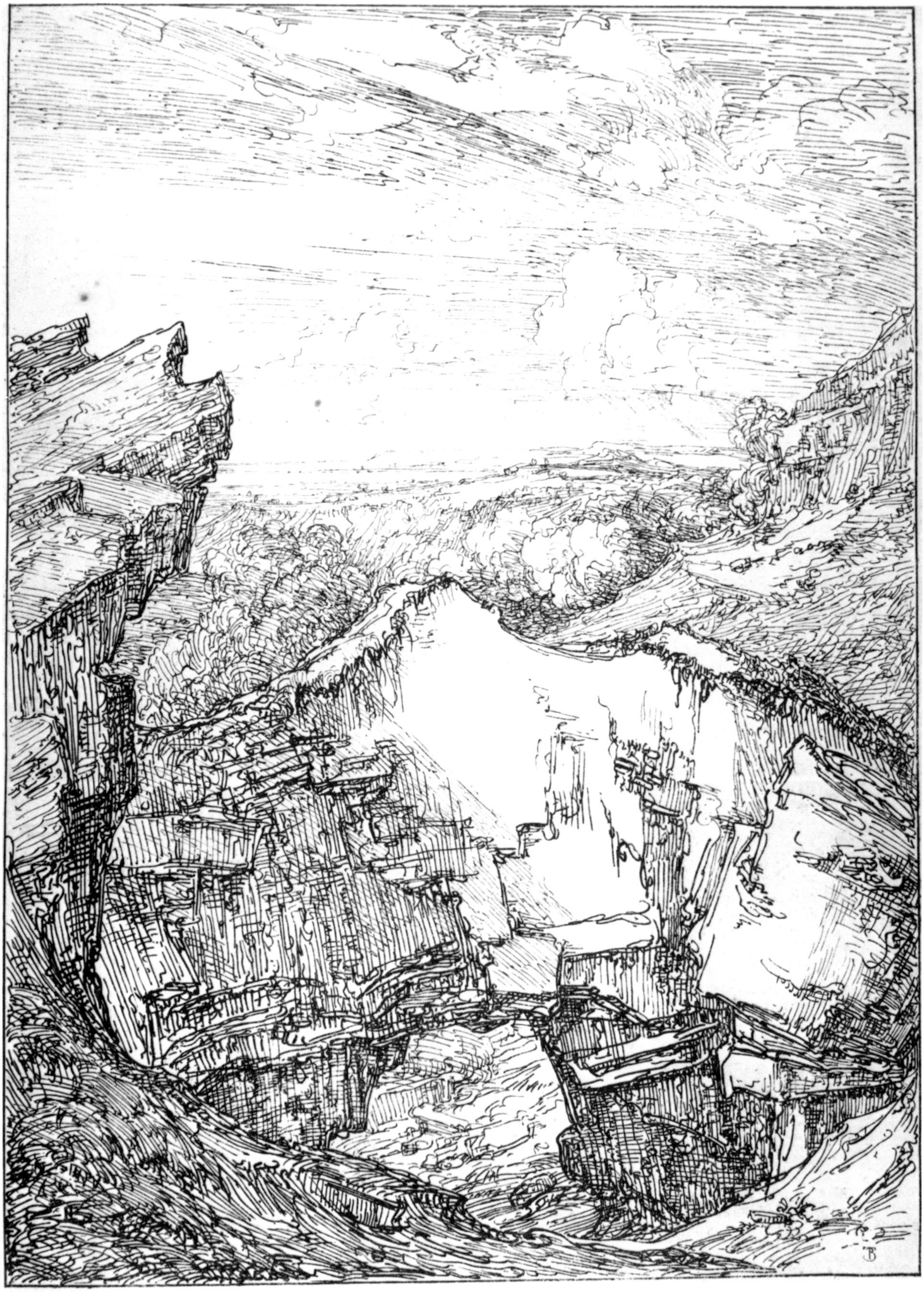

42. Thomas Barker (Barker of Bath), *A Study from Hampton-Down, near Bath,* 1814 (cat. 111)

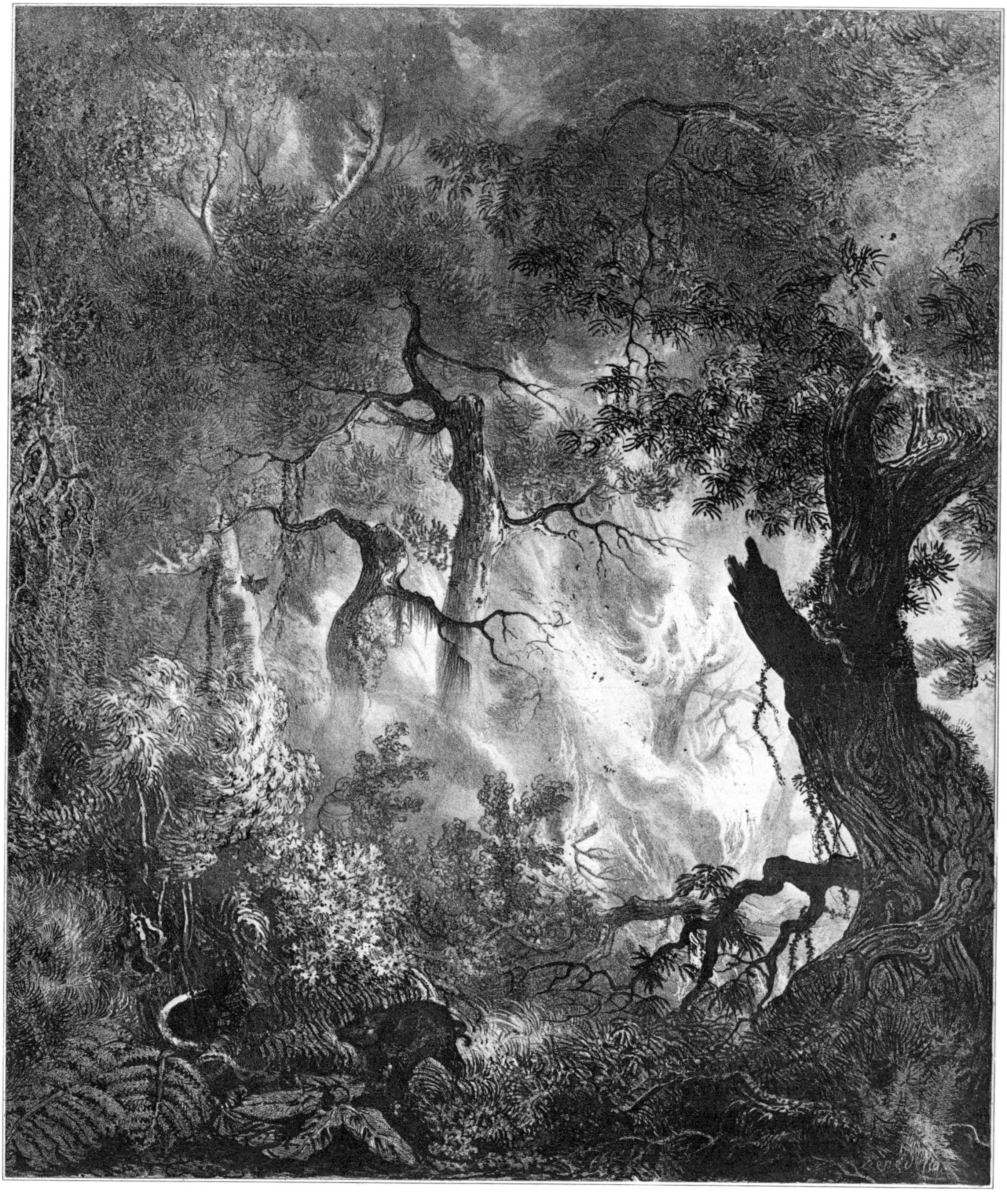

43. Cesare della Chiesa di Benevello, *Spontaneous Combustion of a Forest near Volterra in 1829* (cat. 61)

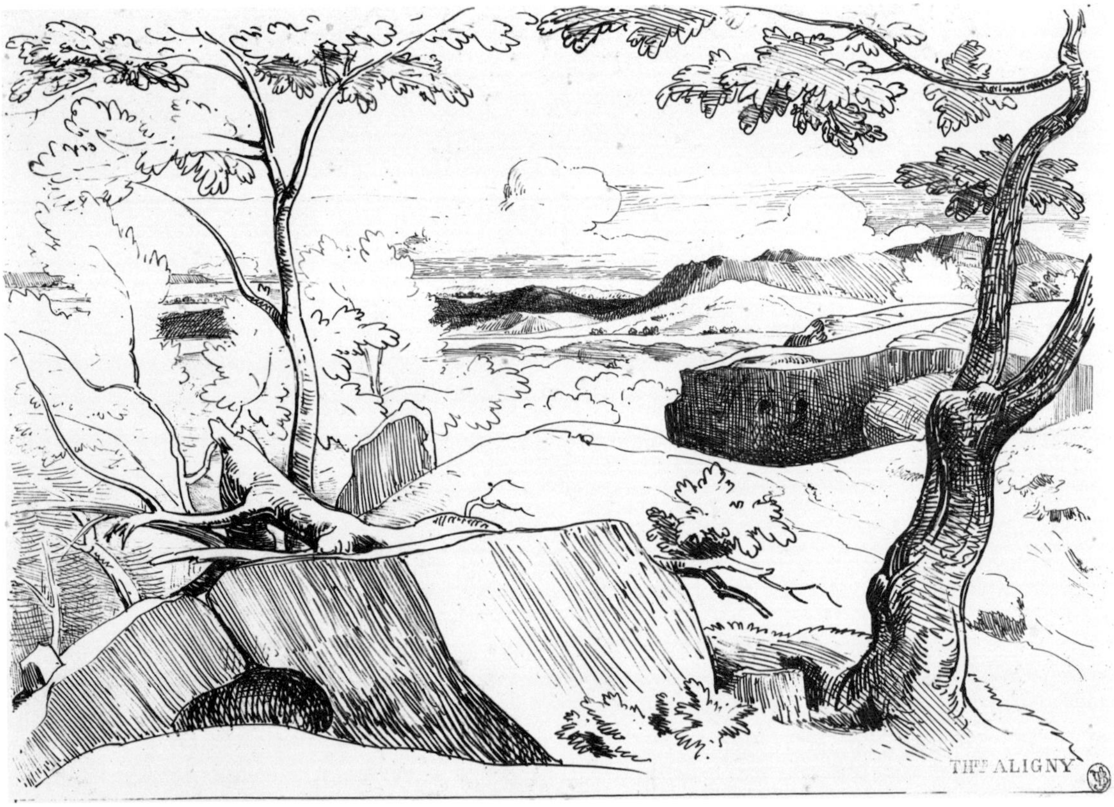

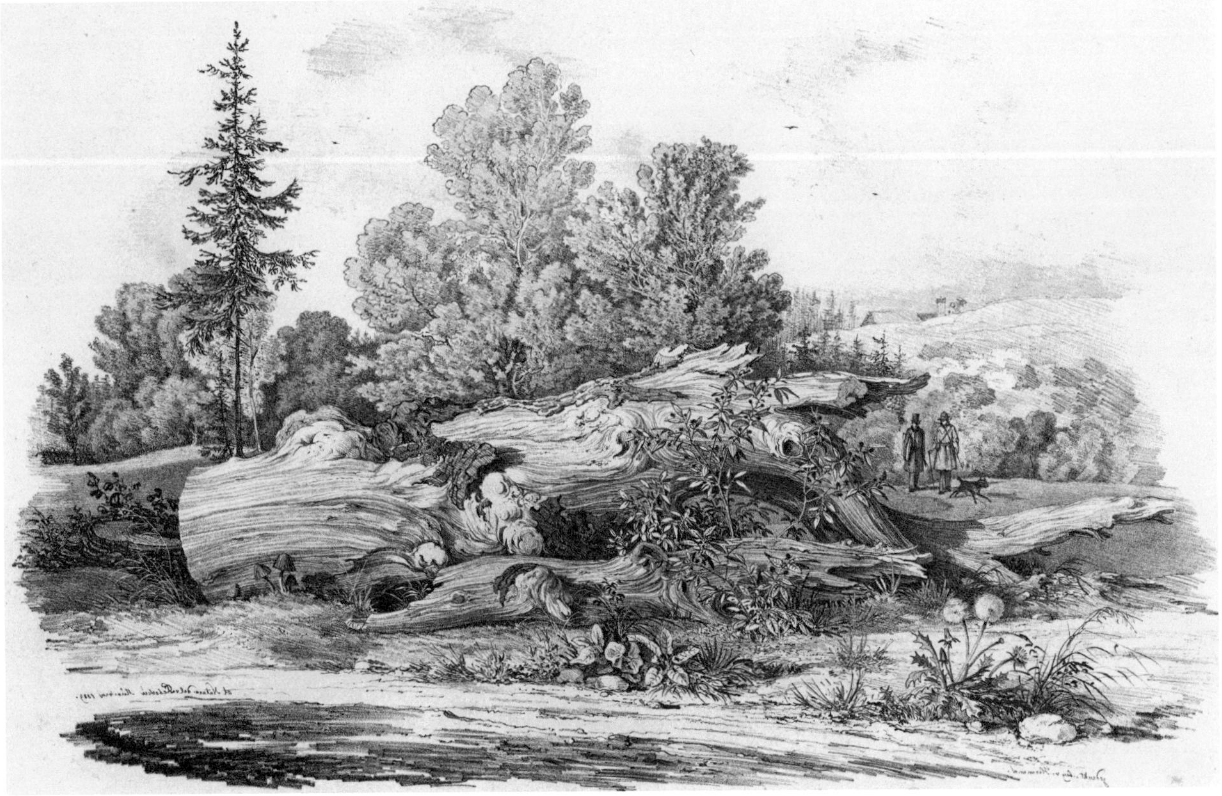

44. Théodore Caruelle d'Aligny, *Rocky Landscape*, probably about 1835 (cat. 66)

45. Carl August Lebschée, *Landscape Vignette with Fallen Tree*, 1829 (cat. 70)

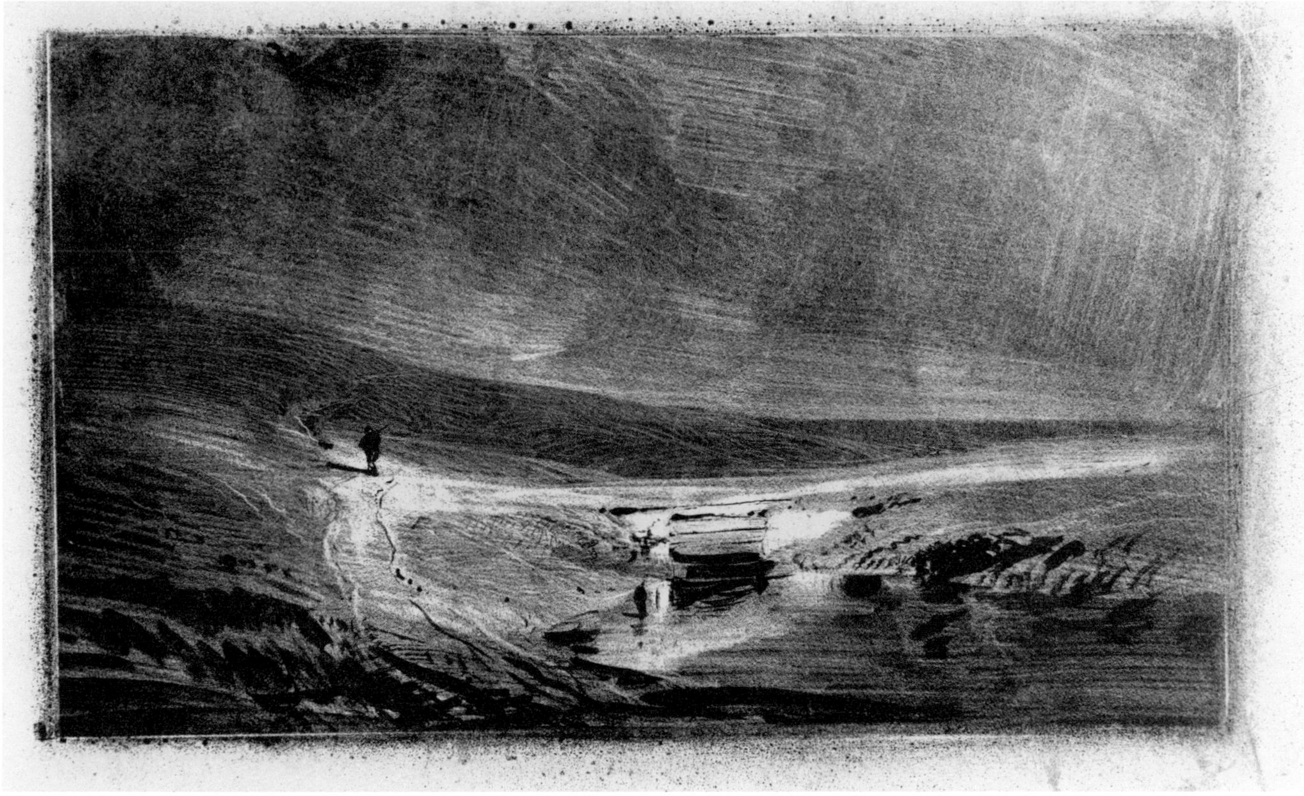

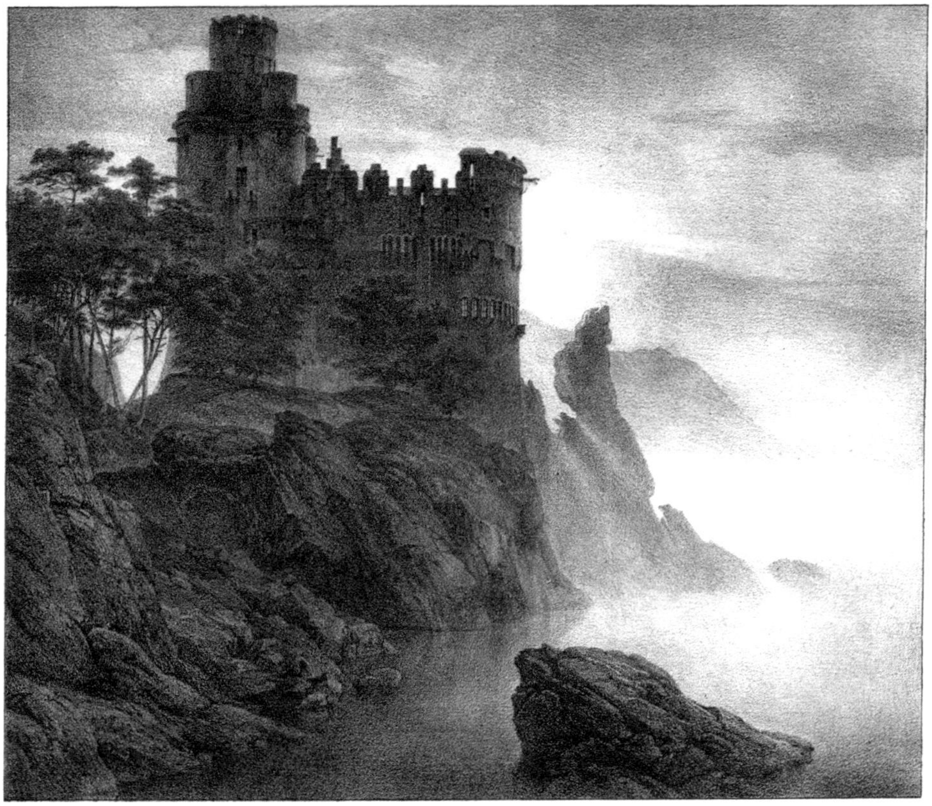

46. Eugène Isabey, *Stormy Weather*, about 1836 (cat. 65)

47. Karl Friedrich Lessing, *Moonlit Landscape with Castle near Water*, probably 1820s or 30s (cat. 60)

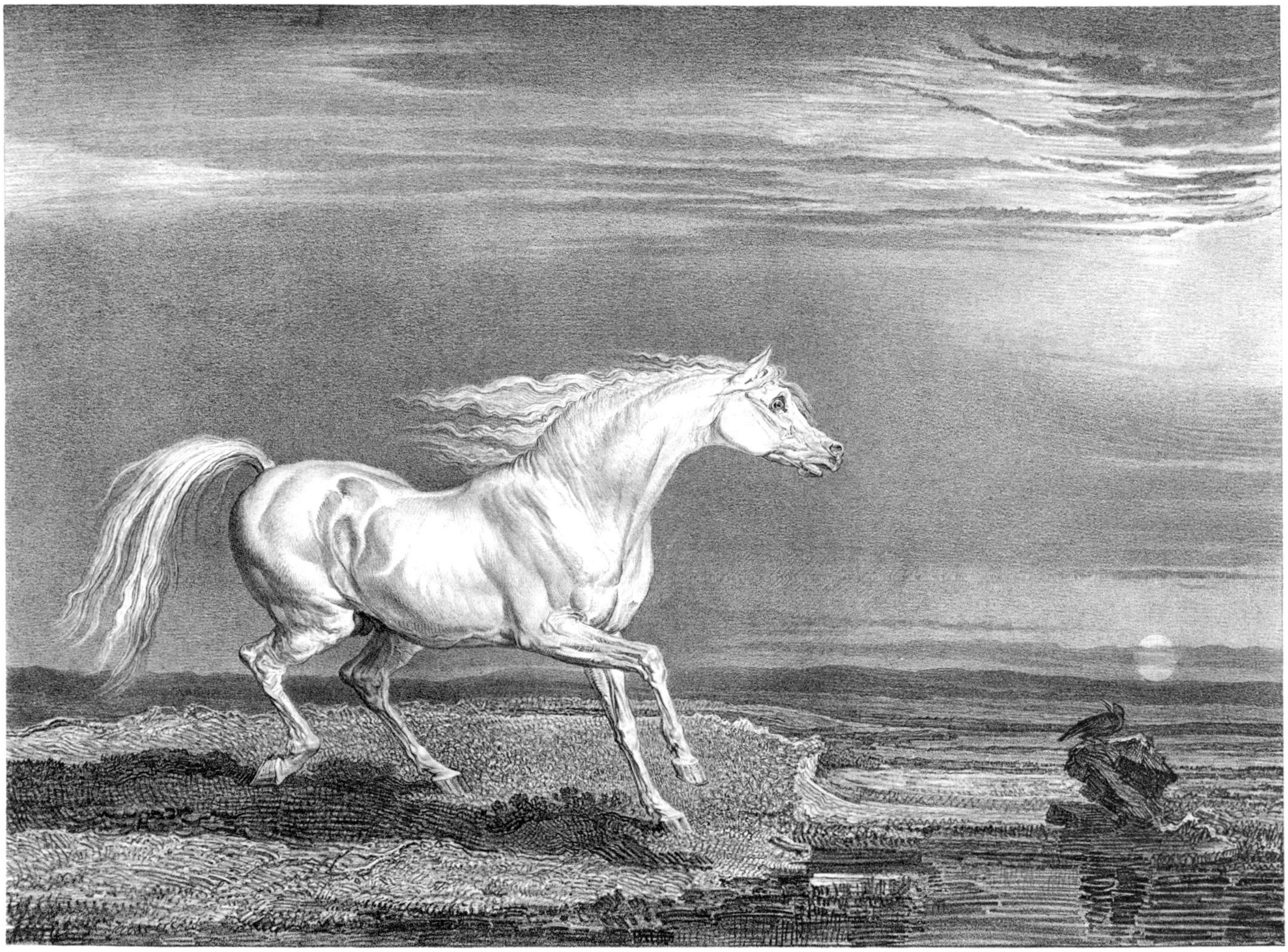

48. James Ward, *Marengo*, 1824 (cat. 3)

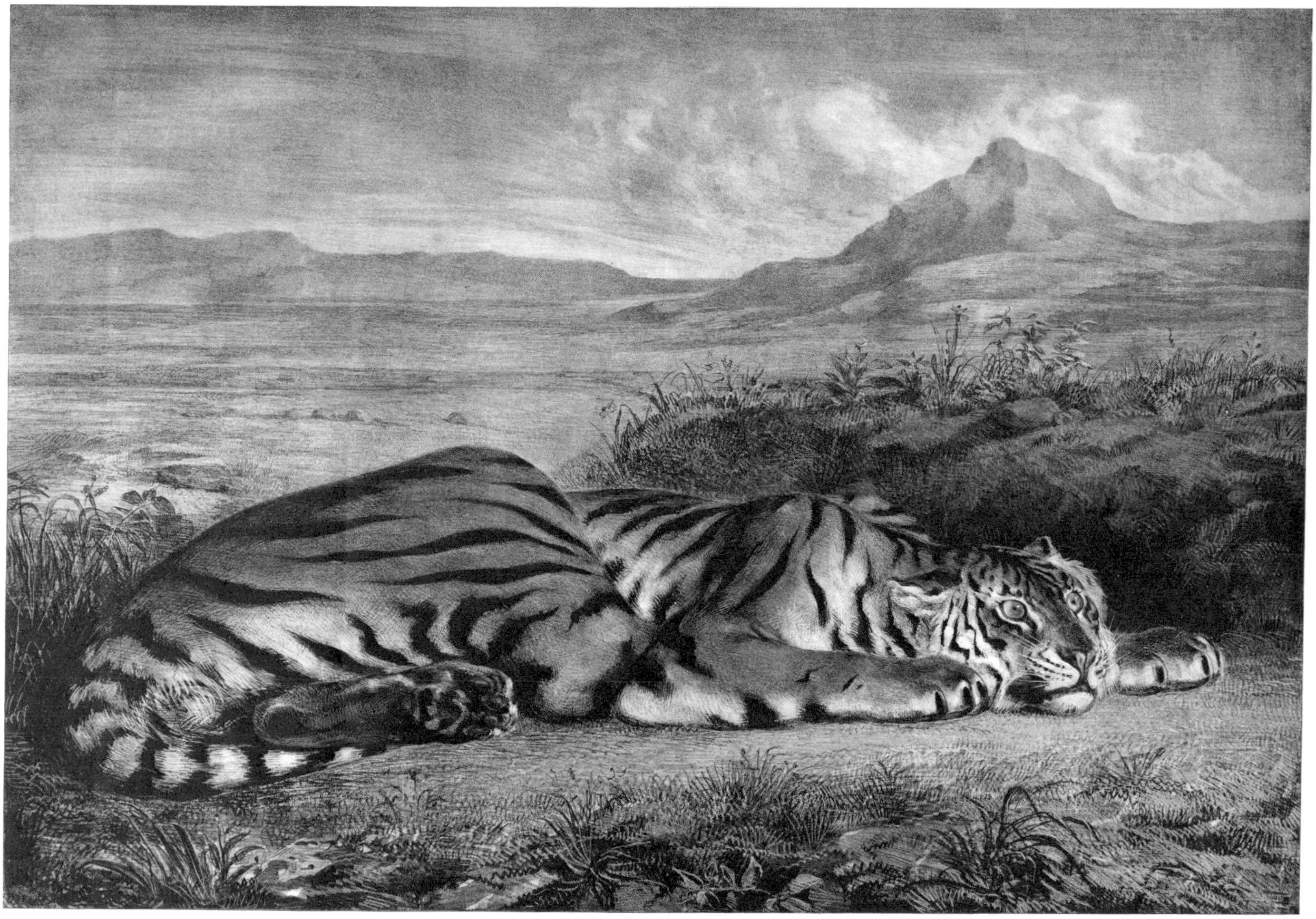

49. Eugène Delacroix, *Royal Tiger*, 1829 (cat. 1)

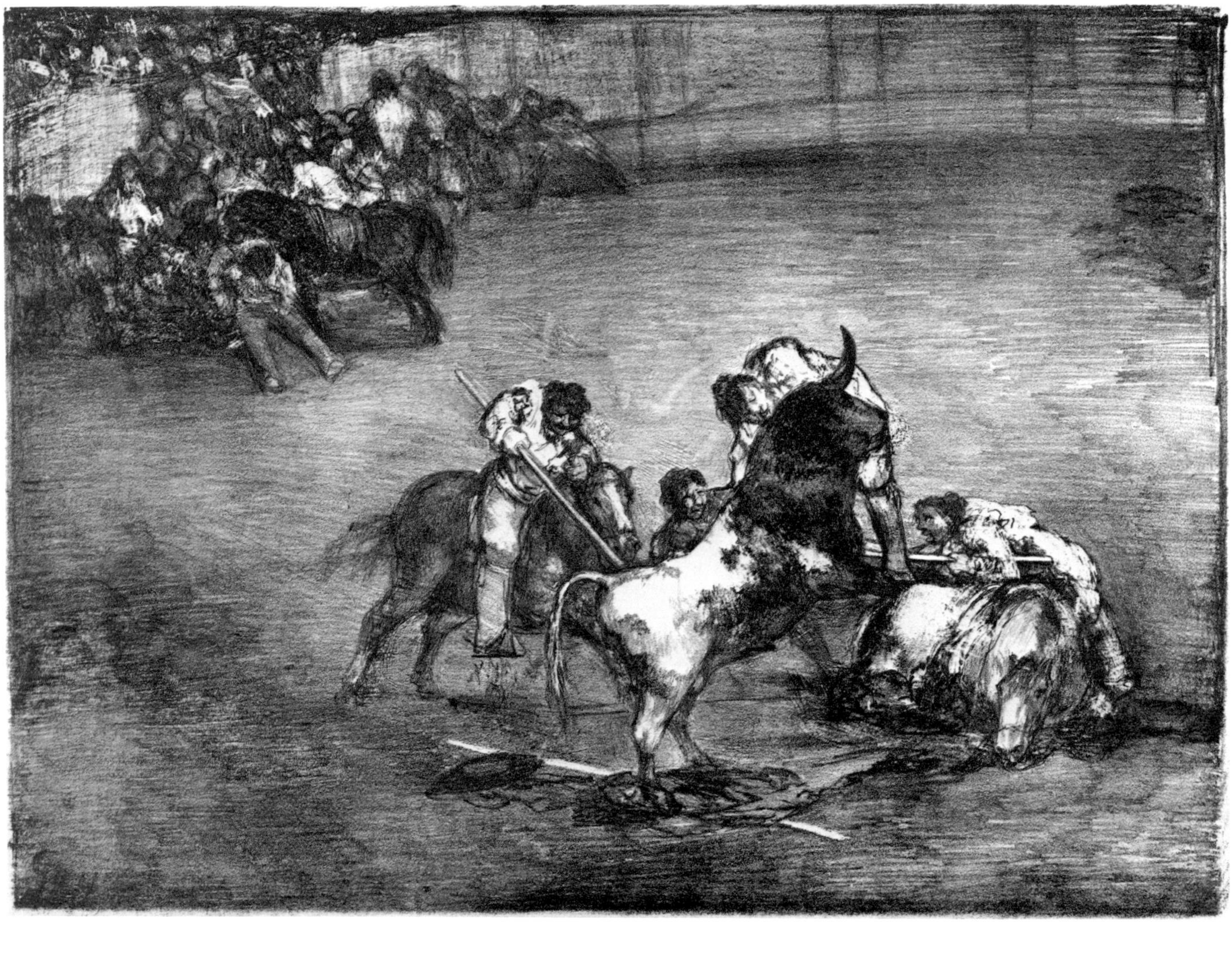

50. Francisco Goya, *Bravo Toro*, 1825 (cat. 79)

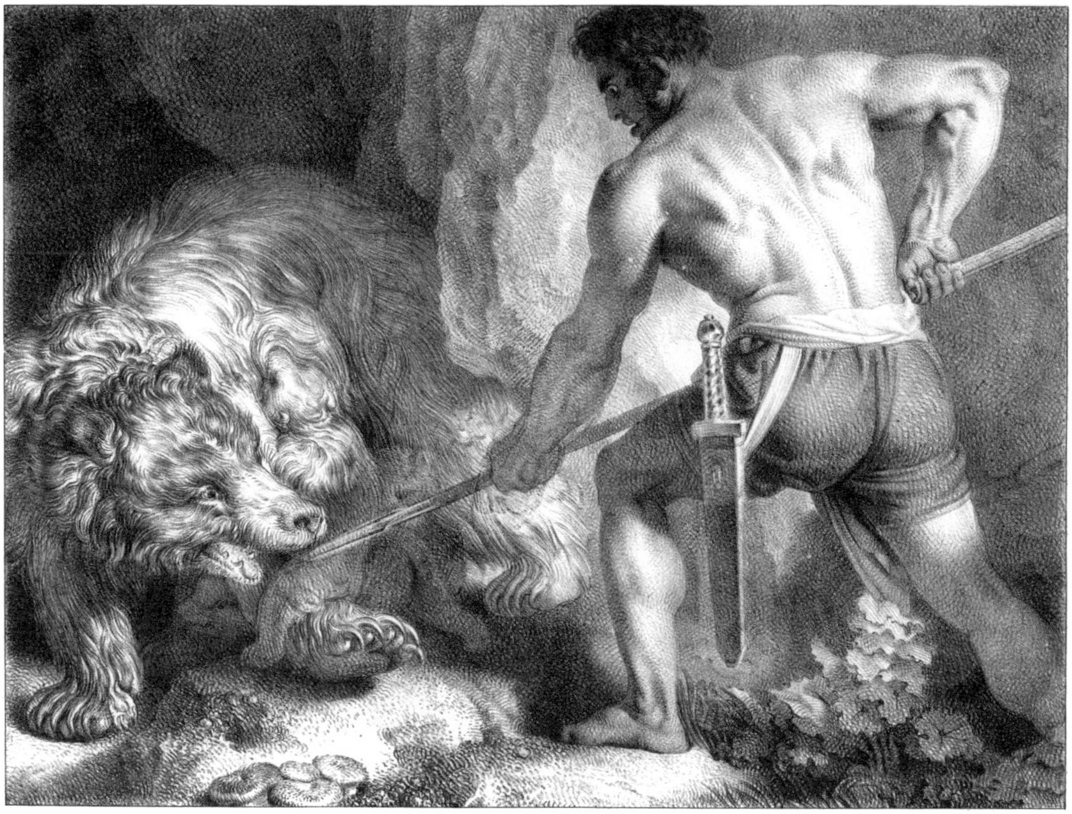

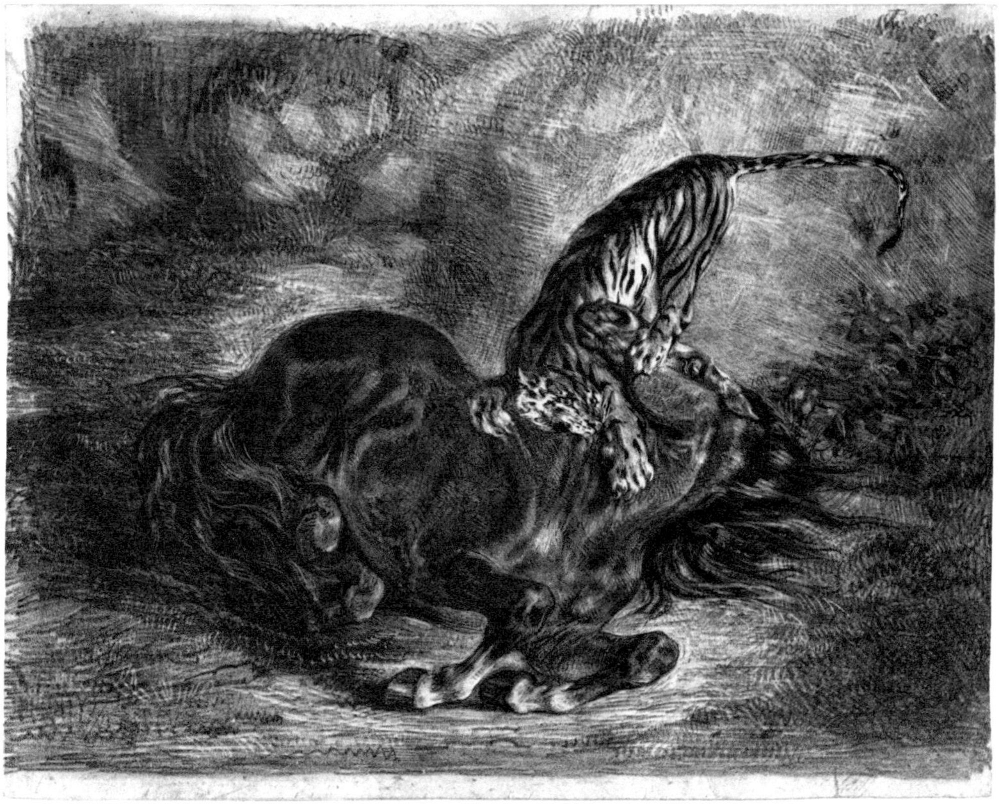

51. Luigi Sabatelli, *The Bear Hunter*, about 1820 (cat. 82)

52. Eugène Delacroix, *Wild Horse Brought Down by a Tiger*, 1828 (cat. 81)

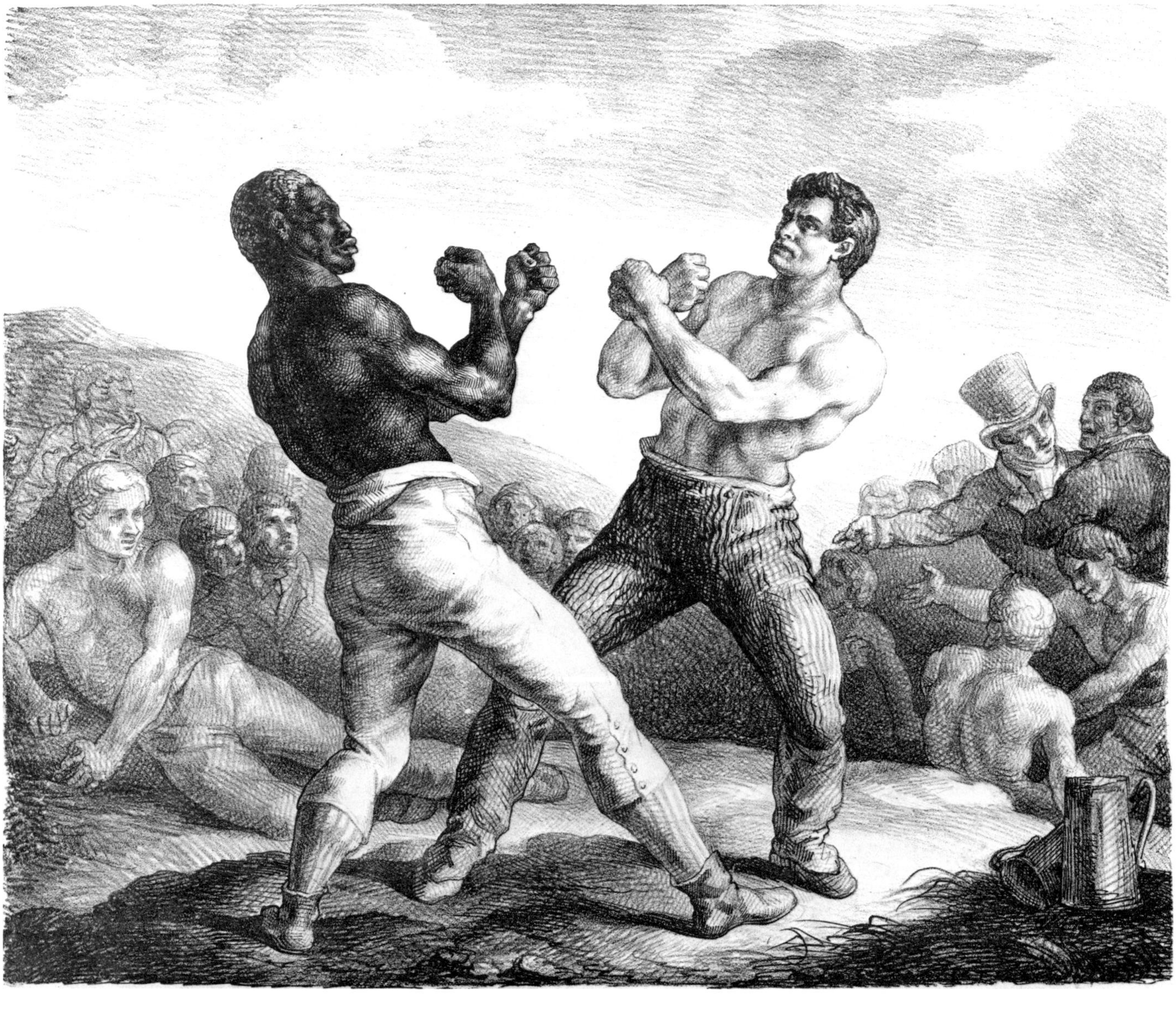

53. Théodore Géricault, *The Boxers*, 1818 (cat. 75)

CHECKLIST OF THE EXHIBITION

Titles of individual prints have been translated from the original language or are descriptive titles, often based on published catalogues. Verses and inscriptions printed beneath the image have not been transcribed or reproduced here. Measurements are of the image only. The checklist reproduces the installation sequence of the exhibition. The exhibition is arranged thematically for comparison and contrast of treatment of subject, style, and technique rather than by chronology or national schools.

Foyer

1. (plate 49)
Eugène Delacroix
(Painter and printmaker)
French, 1798–1863
Royal Tiger, 1829
Lithograph: crayon, brush, and scraping
12¾ x 18¼ in.
Printed and published by H. Gaugain, Paris
Otis Norcross Fund, 1941 M25441

2.
Carle Vernet
(Painter and printmaker)
French, 1758–1836
Pegasus, 1820s
Crayon lithograph
10⅛ x 12 in.
Printed by F. Delpech, Paris; signed in stone: Carle Vernet Rome
Katherine E. Bullard Fund in Memory of Francis Bullard 1995.632

3. (plate 48)
James Ward
(Painter and printmaker)
English, 1769–1859
Marengo, 1824
One of a series of lithographs of celebrated horses
Crayon lithograph
13⅜ x 18 in.
Printed by P. Simons; published by Ward and Rudolph Ackermann, London
Lee M. Friedman Fund 1982.237

First gallery

4. (plate 1)
Nicolas Henri Jacob
(Painter and printmaker)
French, 1782–1871
The Genius of the Invention of Lithography, 1819
Illustration for Aloys Senefelder, *L'Art de la Lithographie*, Paris, Senefelder, 1819
Lithograph: crayon, brush, and scraping
7½ x 6⅜ in.
Katherine E. Bullard Fund in Memory of Francis Bullard 1995.589

5. (plate 3)
Nicolas Toussaint Charlet
(Painter and printmaker)
French, 1792–1845
The Seller of Lithographic Drawings, about 1819
Crayon lithograph
8½ x 12⅛ in.
Printed and published by F. Delpech, Paris
Gift of W. G. Russell Allen 1939.564

6.
Carle Vernet
(Painter and printmaker)
French, 1758–1836
The Lithography Shop of François Delpech, 1818
Crayon lithograph
6⅝ x 9⅝ in.
Printed and published by F. Delpech, Paris
Gift of W. G. Russell Allen 1939.565

7.
Pierre Nolasque Bergeret
(Painter and printmaker)
French, 1782–1863
Martinet's Shop—Dawdlers of the Rue du Coq, 1804
Pen lithograph on greenish paper, hand-colored
8½ x 14¾ in.
Printed by Fr. André, Paris
Katherine E. Bullard Fund in Memory of Francis Bullard 1995.529

8. (plate 2)
Honoré Daumier
(Painter, sculptor, and printmaker)
French, 1808–1879
Two Men Reading Le Charivari, 1840
Crayon lithograph
8½ x 9 in.
Published in *Le Charivari*, April 1, 1840
Bequest of William P. Babcock, 1900
B4279

9.
Thomas Shotter Boys
(Watercolorist and printmaker)
English, 1803–1874
Hôtel de Cluny, 1839
From the series *Picturesque Architecture in Paris, Ghent, Antwerp, Rouen . . .*
Crayon lithograph printed in color
10¾ x 9 in.
Printed by C. Hullmandel, London; published by Boys
Bequest of W.P.P. Longfellow, 1913
M25042

10.
Carle Vernet
(Painter and printmaker)
French, 1758–1836
Balancing the Glass, 1823
Crayon lithograph
8⅝ x 10¾ in.
Printed by F. Delpech, Paris
Gift of W. G. Russell Allen 1938.621

11. (plate 9)
Théodore Géricault
(Painter, sculptor, and printmaker)
French, 1791–1824
The Sleeping Fish Merchant, 1820
Pen lithograph, printed from stone paper
8½ x 11½ in.
Frederick Keppel Memorial Bequest, 1913 M23502

12. (plate 12)
Théodore Géricault
(Painter, printmaker, and sculptor)
French, 1791–1824
Entrance to the Adelphi Wharf, 1821
From *Various Subjects Drawn from Life and on the Stone*, London, 1821
Crayon lithograph
10 x 12⅛ in.
Printed by Charles Hullmandel, published by Rodwell and Martin
Gift of W. G. Russell Allen 1960.372

13. (plate 19)
Paul Huet
(Painter and printmaker)
French, 1803–1869
Full and Total Amnesty Granted by Death in 1832
Crayon lithograph
10 x 14 in.

Printed by Becquet, Paris; published in *La Caricature*, Nov. 8, 1832, based on an idea suggested by the publisher, Charles Philipon.
Bequest of William P. Babcock, 1900
B4013

14. (plate 18)
Alexandre Gabriel Decamps
(Painter and printmaker)
French, 1803–1860
Year of Grace 1840, in the Glorious Reign of Charles X (extract from the court circular of the ex-king), 1830
Crayon lithograph, with scraping
8 x 13½ in.
Published by Gihaut frères, Paris, August 29, 1830
Gift of William Norton Bullard
1923.1094

15.
Honoré Daumier
(Painter, sculptor, and printmaker)
French, 1808–1879
Rue Transnonain, 15 April, 1834
Crayon lithograph, with scraping
11¼ x 17⅜ in.
Printed by Delaunois, Paris; published in *L'Association mensuelle pour la liberté de la presse*, July, 1834
Bequest of William P. Babcock, 1900
B4302

16. (plate 6)
Louis Lecoeur
(Printmaker)
French, active about 1784–1825
The Plaything of the Moment (Le Joujou du Jour), about 1815
Crayon lithograph
8⅝ x 11½ in.
Printed by C. Motte; published by Martinet, Paris
William A. Sargent Fund 1954.1052

17. (plate 10)
Jean Baptiste Isabey
(Miniaturist and printmaker)
French, 1767–1855
Arrival of His Royal Highness, the Duke of Bordeaux, at Chambord, 1821
Lithograph: crayon and pen
12⅛ x 17¾ in.
Printed by C. Motte, Paris; published by Isabey
George R. Nutter Fund 1995.135

18. (plate 7)
Honoré Daumier
(Painter, sculptor, and printmaker)
French, 1808–1879
The Legislative Belly, View of the Ministers' Benches in the Unprostituted Chamber of 1834
Lithograph: crayon and brush
11 x 17 in.
Printed by Becquet, Paris; published by Aubert in *L'Association mensuelle pour la liberté de la presse*, January, 1834
Bequest of William P. Babcock, 1900
B4299

19.
Anne Louis Girodet-Trioson
(Painter, writer, and printmaker)
French, 1767–1824
Portrait of the Artist Marie Philippe Coupin de la Couperie, 1816
Crayon lithograph
8¾ x 7¼ in.
Printed by G. Engelmann, Paris
Harvey D. Parker Collection, 1897
P18071

20. (plate 13)
Jean Baptiste Chometon
(Painter and printmaker)
French, 1789–after 1831
The Artist's Mother and Sister, 1819
Crayon lithograph
6½ x 7½ in.
Printed by François Villain, Paris
Gift of W. G. Russell Allen 1938.303

21.
Attributed to Jacques Antoine Marie Lemoine (signed in stone: Lemoine)
(Painter and miniaturist)
French, 1751–1824
Portrait of a Man with Spectacles; Various Portrait Sketches at Left, 1819
Crayon lithograph
7½ x 7⅞ in.
Gift of Samuel P. Avery, 1888 M5833

22.
Jean Marie Jacomin
(Painter and printmaker)
French, 1789–1858
The Artist and his Friends, 1821
Crayon lithograph
5⅝ x 13 in.
Printed and published by G. Engelmann, Paris
Gift of William S. Appleton, 1893
M9262

23.
Alexandre Marie Colin
(Painter and printmaker)
French, 1798–1875
The Painter Girodet-Trioson and his Pupils, about 1817
Crayon lithograph
7¼ x 10¾ in.
Fund in Memory of Horatio Greenough Curtis 1983.266

24. (plate 8)
Johann Gottfried Schadow
(Sculptor and printmaker)
German, 1764–1850
Portrait of the Artist's Brother, the Accountant Rudolf Schadow, 1824
Crayon lithograph with tan tint stone
11 x 6¾ in.
George R. Nutter Fund 1959.748

25. (plate 20)
Anonymous, Italian (Milan)
The Empress Marie Louise (wife of Napoleon I), 1811–12
Crayon lithograph
6½ x 5 in.
Probably printed and published by De Werz, Milan
Katherine E. Bullard Fund in Memory of Francis Bullard 1995.192

26. (plate 4)
Joseph Dionysius Odevaere
(Painter and printmaker)
Belgian, 1778–1830
Self-portrait, 1816
Crayon lithograph
13½ x 9⅞ in.
Printed by G.Engelmann, Paris
Gift of W. G. Russell Allen, 1938
M34700

27.
Paul Gavarni (Guillaume Sulpice Chevallier)
(Watercolorist, writer, and printmaker)
French, 1804–1866
Self-portrait, 1842
Lithograph: crayon and brush, with scraping, on thin gray paper mounted during printing
7⅜ x 5½ in.
Printed by Bertauts, Paris
Louis Curtis Fund 1937.101

28.
Paul Gavarni (Guillaume Sulpice Chevallier)

(Watercolorist, printmaker, and writer)
French, 1804–1866
Lithographic stone from which the self-portrait (no. 27) was printed
13¾ x 10⅝ x 1⅜ in.
Maria Antoinette Evans Fund 1930.1203

29. (plate 5)
Achille Devéria
(Painter and printmaker)
French, 1800–1857
Self-portrait ("à l'air fatal"), 1830
Crayon lithograph on thin gray paper mounted during printing
15¾ x 11⅜ in.
Lee M. Friedman Fund 1984.417

30. (plate 21)
Eugène Delacroix
(Painter and printmaker)
French, 1798–1863
Baron Schwiter (at age 21), 1826
Crayon lithograph with scraping
8⅝ x 7⅝ in.
Lee M. Friedman Fund 1963.1011

31.
Eugène Delacroix
(Painter and printmaker)
French, 1798–1863
Hamlet sees the Ghost of his Father, 1843
From a series (1834–43) of scenes from Shakespeare's *Hamlet*
Crayon lithograph with scraping
10¼ x 7½ in.
Printed by Bertauts, Paris, 1864
Bequest of William P. Babcock, 1900 B1227

32. (plate 24)
Francesco Hayez
(Painter and printmaker)
Italian, 1791–1882
"Turn, false-hearted Templar," 1834
From a series (1828–34) of scenes from Sir Walter Scott's novel *Ivanhoe*
Crayon lithograph with scraping
13⅛ x 15¾ in.
Printed by Vassalli, Milan
Katherine E. Bullard Fund in Memory of Francis Bullard 1995.366(a)

33.
Francesco Hayez
(Painter and printmaker)
Italian, 1791–1882
Pagano and Gulfiero Bearing the Body of Giselda, about 1826
Illustration to Tommaso Grossi's epic poem "I Lombardi alla prima crociata" (The Lombards at the First Crusade), 1826, Canto 13
Crayon lithograph with scraping
11½ x 16½ in.
Printed by Elena, Milan
Katherine E. Bullard Fund in Memory of Francis Bullard 1995.347

34. (plate 23)
Eugène Delacroix
(Painter and printmaker)
French, 1798–1863
Faust and Mephistopheles galloping on the Night of the Witches' Sabbath, 1826–27
For the illustrated edition of Goethe's play *Faust*, published by C. Motte, Paris, 1828.
Crayon lithograph with scraping, on thin paper mounted during printing. Early proof with marginal lithographic sketches.
9⅜ x 12¼ in.
Lee M. Friedman Fund 1963.1012

35.
Narcisse Diaz de la Peña
(Painter and printmaker)
French, 1808–1876
Imposture!, about 1844
One of six lithographs originally made to accompany the romantic fantasy "Les Visions de Quevedo"
Crayon lithograph on thin cream paper mounted during printing
8⅜ x 6¼ in.
Printed by Bertauts; published by Bouvenne, Paris
Bequest of William P. Babcock, 1900 B1270

36.
Adolf Menzel
(Painter and printmaker)
German, 1815–1905
The Pursuit, 1851
From the series *Versuche auf Stein mit Pinsel und Schabeisen* (Experiments on Stone with Brush and Scraper), 1851
Lithograph: crayon and brush, with scraping, and tan tint stone on thin paper mounted during printing
8⅛ x 5¾ in.
Printed by J. Hesse, Berlin
Harvey D. Parker Fund, 1912 M22084

37. (plate 26)
Francisco Goya
(Painter and printmaker)
Spanish, 1746–1828
Woman Asleep or in a Trance, probably 1819–22
Crayon lithograph
5¼ x 6⅜ in.
Probably printed by José Maria Cardano at the Hydrographic Bureau, Madrid
Katherine E. Bullard Fund in Memory of Francis Bullard and Gift of Landon T. Clay 1971.622

38. (plate 27)
Jean Auguste Dominique Ingres
(Painter and printmaker)
French, 1780–1867
Odalisque, 1825
Crayon lithograph
5⅛ x 8⅜ in.
Printed and published by F. Delpech, Paris
Bequest of W.G. Russell Allen 1960.600

39. (plate 32)
Giuseppe Longhi
(Miniaturist and printmaker)
Italian, 1766–1831
Susanna and the Elders, 1821
Crayon lithograph in brown ink
6 x 10 in.
Printed in Milan
Katherine E. Bullard Fund in Memory of Francis Bullard 1995.413

40. (plate 28)
Henry Fuseli
(Painter and printmaker)
Swiss, 1741–1825
"Evening thou bringest all" (Woman at a Window), 1802
From *Specimens of Polyautography*, second issue, published by G.J. Vollweiler, London, 1806
Pen lithograph
9⅛ x 12⅝ in.
Gift of W.G. Russell Allen 1941.164

41.
Anonymous, Italian (Milan, circle of Andrea Appiani)
Woman in Antique Dress Reclining in a Landscape, 1815–18
Lithograph: crayon and pen in brownish ink
4⅛ x 8⅞ in.
Katherine E. Bullard Fund in Memory of Francis Bullard 1995.197

42. (plate 25)
Pierre Paul Prud'hon
(Painter and printmaker)
French, 1758–1823
Reading (Une Lecture), 1822
Crayon lithograph
7⅛ x 5¾ in.
Printed by C. Motte, Paris
Bequest of William P. Babcock, 1900
B3133

43. (plate 29)
Théodore Chassériau
(Painter and printmaker)
French, 1819–1856
Venus Rising from the Sea, 1839
Crayon lithograph with scraping and tan tint stone
12⅛ x 11⅛ in.
Printed by Auguste Bry; published by Goupil and Vibert, Paris
Gift of W.G. Russell Allen 1950.3459

44. (plate 31)
Anne Louis Girodet-Trioson
(Painter, printmaker, and writer)
French, 1767–1824
The Bard Armin Lamenting the Death of his Children, about 1816
A scene from the epic poems of the "ancient Celtic bard" Ossian (a literary forgery by the Scottish poet James Macpherson)
Crayon lithograph
7 x 8¼ in.
Probably printed by G. Engelmann, Paris
Harvey D. Parker Collection, 1897
P18070

45. (plate 30)
Pierre Nolasque Bergeret
(Painter and printmaker)
French, 1782–1863
Deathbed Scene in Antiquity, about 1804–05
Crayon lithograph
7¼ x 10½ in.
Helen and Alice Colburn Fund 1958.789

46.
Eugène Delacroix
(Painter and printmaker)
French, 1798–1863
Hercules and Antaeus, 1847–49
Pen lithograph from transfer paper
10⅜ x 17⅛ in.
Printed by Bertauts, Paris
Lee M. Friedman Fund 1987.299

47. (plate 33)
Joshua Cristall
(Painter and printmaker)
English, 1767/69–1847
Apollo and the Muses, 1816
Pen lithograph
13⅛ x 17¾ in.
Published by the artist
Lee M. Friedman Fund 1983.506

48. (plate 22)
Benjamin West
(Painter and printmaker)
American (active England), 1738–1820
Angel of the Resurrection, 1801
From *Specimens of Polyautography*, second issue,published by G.J. Vollweiler, London, 1806
Pen lithograph
12⅞ x 9 in.
Gift of W.G. Russell Allen 1941.167

49.
Ludwig Wolf
(Painter and printmaker)
German, 1776–1832
Hero and Leander, 1818
Pen lithograph with brown tint stone
15¼ x 12½ in.
Printed and published by F. W. Reuter, Berlin. This was to be number one in a new series, *Polyautographische Zeichnungen der vorzüglichsten Europäischen Künstler unseres Zeitalters* (Polyautographic Drawings by the Most Outstanding European Artists of Our Time), the never-issued successor to Reuter's 1805 series *Polyautographische Zeichnungen vorzüglicher Berliner Künstler* (Polyautographic Drawings by Outstanding Berlin Artists).
Gift of W.G. Russell Allen 1938.652

Case

50.
James Barry
(Painter and printmaker)
English, 1741–1806
Eastern Patriarch, 1803
In *Specimens of Polyautography consisting of Impressions taken from Original Drawings made on stone purposely for this work*, published by G.J. Vollweiler, London, 1806
Pen lithograph
9¼ x 12½ in.
Gift of W. G. Russell Allen 1941.164

51.
Alexandre Evariste Fragonard
(Painter, sculptor, and printmaker)
French, 1780–1850
Ruins of the Chateau of Tancarville, 1821
Plate 41 in Ch. Nodier, J. Taylor and Alph. De Cailleux, *Voyages pittoresques et romantiques dans l'ancienne France*, Normandy, vol. l, Paris, 1820
Crayon lithograph on thin cream paper mounted during printing
14½ x 10 in.
Printed by G. Engelmann
Anonymous Gift

52.
Eugène Delacroix
(Painter and printmaker)
French, 1798–1863
Vercingétorix, 1829
Historical endpiece for Ch. Nodier, J. Taylor and Alph. De Cailleux, *Voyages pittoresques et romantiques dans l'ancienne France*, Auvergne, vol. 1, Paris, 1829
Crayon lithograph
9¾ x 7¼ in.
Printed by G. Engelmann
Bequest of W.G. Russell Allen 1960.270

Second gallery

53.
Simon Petrus Klotz
(Painter and printmaker)
German, 1776–1824
Part of the Ruins of the Villa of Maecenas, Tivoli, 1807
Crayon lithograph
10¼ x 14⅛ in.
Gift of W.G. Russell Allen 1938.482

54.
Domenico Quaglio II
(Painter and printmaker)
German, 1787–1837
Saint Margaret's Chapel in the Castle, Nuremberg, 1819
From a series on medieval German architecture, *Sammlung denkwürdiger Gebäude des Mittelalters in Deutschland*
Crayon lithograph with scraping and brown tint stone
14⅛ x 15¼ in.
Stephen Bullard Memorial Fund 1993.876

55.
Friedrich von Gaertner
(Architect, painter, and printmaker)
German, 1792–1847

Antique Fragments, 1818
From a series of lithographs by Bavarian artists, *Original-Handzeichnungen bayrischen Künstler*
Crayon lithograph with tan tint stone
10⅞ x 14⅝ in.
Published by J. G. Zeller, Munich
Lee M. Friedman Fund 1986.384

56. (plate 41)
Giovanni Migliara
(Painter and printmaker)
Italian, 1785–1837
after a design by Gaspare Galliari
(scenic designer and painter)
Italian, 1761–1823
Monumental Arch, 1808–10
Crayon lithograph
9¼ x 7⅛ in.
Printed by De Werz, Milan
Katherine E. Bullard Fund in Memory of Francis Bullard 1995.287

57. (plate 40)
Richard Parkes Bonington
(Painter and printmaker)
English (active France), 1802–1828
Remains of a Gothic Doorway, 1824
Proof before letters of the rejected version of the title page for the series, *Restes et fragments d'architecture*
Crayon lithograph
7 x 4⅞ in.
Probably printed by Feillet, Paris
Samuel P. Avery Fund 1921.10768

58.
Samuel Prout
(Painter and printmaker)
English, 1783–1852
Part of the Cathedral, Rouen, 1821
Crayon lithograph
14⅝ x 11½ in.
Printed by C. Hullmandel; published by Rodwell & Martin, London
Gift of Paul J. Sachs, 1913 M22516

59.
Carl Blechen
(Painter and printmaker)
Germany, 1798–1840
The Flight into Egypt, 1828
Crayon lithograph
9¼ x 13½ in.
Lee M. Friedman Fund 1991.702

60. (plate 47)
Karl Friedrich Lessing
(Painter and printmaker)
Germany, born Poland, 1808–1880
Moonlit Landscape with Castle near Water, probably 1820s or 30s
Crayon lithograph
9⅛ x 10½ in.
Printed by I.B. Hützer, Cologne
Lee M. Friedman Fund 1986.365

61. (plate 43)
Cesare della Chiesa di Benevello
(Patron of the arts, painter, and printmaker)
Italian, 1788–1853
Spontaneous Combustion of a Forest near Volterra in 1829
Lithograph: crayon and brush with spatter and scraping
18⅛ x 15⅛ in.
Printed by D. Festa, Turin
Katherine E. Bullard Fund in Memory of Francis Bullard 1995.213

62.
François Joseph Pfeiffer II
(Painter and printmaker)
Dutch, 1778–1835
Man Standing among Gnarled Trees, 1817
From a series of six tree studies
Crayon lithograph
12¾ x 8⅞ in.
Printed by Beyer and Vinkeles, Amsterdam
Lee M. Friedman Fund 1986.381

63.
Raphael Lamar West
(Painter and printmaker)
English, 1769–1850
Ancient Oak with Seated Man, 1802
Other impressions included in *Specimens of Polyautography*, second issue, published by G.J. Vollweiler, London, 1806
Pen lithograph on gray-brown paper
12⅛ x 8⅞ in.
Museum Purchase, 1894 M9844

64.
Jules Dupré
(Painter and printmaker)
French, 1811–1889
Banks of the Somme (Picardy), about 1836
Crayon lithograph
5⅜ x 8⅜ in.
Printed by Bénard & Frey; published in the art journal *L'Artiste*
Special Print Fund, 1916 M26221

65. (plate 46)
Eugène Isabey
(Painter and printmaker)
French, 1803–1886
Stormy Weather, about 1836
Lithograph: experiment with crayon, brush, and scraping
4⅜ x 7¼ in.
Samuel P. Avery Fund 1921.10733

66. (plate 44)
Théodore Caruelle d'Aligny
(Painter and printmaker)
French, 1798–1871
Rocky Landscape, probably about 1835
Pen lithograph
8¾ x 12 in.
Lee M. Friedman Fund 1985.871

67.
Florent Fidèle Constant Bourgeois du Castelet
(Painter and printmaker)
French, 1767–1841
View of the Oson Bridge, near Tournon, Ardèche, 1818
From a series of 80 plates, *Recueil de vues pittoresques de la France*
Crayon lithograph
8⅝ x 12¼ in.
Printed by C. de Lasteyrie
Gift of W.G. Russell Allen 1938.295

68.
Simon Warnberger
(Painter and printmaker)
German, 1769–1847
Around the Schlier-See (Woman herding Cattle), 1807
Crayon lithograph
8¼ x 11⅞ in.
Gift of W.G. Russell Allen 1938.646

69.
Max Joseph Wagenbauer
(Painter and printmaker)
Germany, 1775–1829
In the Vicinity of Wangen (Landscape with a Horse-Drawn Wagon), 1808
Crayon lithograph on pale green paper
8½ x 12 in.
Fund in Memory of Horatio Greenough Curtis 1962.10

70. (plate 45)
Carl August Lebschée
(Painter and printmaker)
German, 1800–1877
Landscape Vignette with Fallen Tree, 1829

From a portfolio of six landscape prints by Lebschée, *Cahier de différentes études en six feuilles*
Crayon lithograph with scraping
8⅝ x 13¼ in.
Printed and published by I. N. Hermann, Munich
Katherine E. Bullard Fund in Memory of Francis Bullard 1995.659.3

71.
Henry W. Burgess
(Painter and printmaker)
English, active about 1809–1844
Two Trees in an Old Graveyard, about 1815
Crayon lithograph
11⅜ x 14¾ in.
Gift of W.G. Russell Allen 1923.1360

72.
Richard Cooper
(Painter and printmaker)
English, about 1740–1814
Resting Man under Large Tree by a Wooded Bank, 1802
Other impressions included in *Specimens of Polyautography*, published by Ph. André, London, 1803
Pen lithograph
9½ x 13 in.
Gift of W.G. Russell Allen 1923.1376

73.
Antoine Pierre Mongin
(Painter, printmaker, and writer)
French, 1762–1827
Trunks of Chestnut Trees, 1816
From a set of eight tree images, part of the *Cours complet d'études du dessin*
Crayon lithograph
17⅝ x 13¼ in.
Printed by G. Engelmann
George R. Nutter Fund 1956.522

74. (plate 38)
Raphael Lamar West
(Painter and printmaker)
English, 1769–1850
Head of a Bearded Man Wreathed with Oak Branches, 1802
Pen lithograph
10¾ x 8½ in.
Museum Purchase Funds, 1894 M9843

75. (plate 53)
Théodore Géricault
(Painter, sculptor, and printmaker)
France, 1791–1824
The Boxers, 1818
Lithograph: crayon and brush
13⅞ x 16⅜ in.
Printed by C. Motte, Paris
John Wheelock Eliot Fund 1934.575

76.
Eugène Delacroix
(Painter and printmaker)
French, 1798–1863
Frightened Wild Horse Emerging from the Water, 1828
Crayon lithograph with scraping; early proof before letters
9 x 9⅛ in.
Harvey D. Parker Collection, 1897 P18053

77.
Francisco Goya
(Painter and printmaker)
Spanish, 1746–1828
Spanish Diversion, 1825
These four bullfighting images (nos. 77–80) are usually referred to as the "Bulls of Bordeaux"
Crayon lithograph with scraping
12 x 16¼ in.
Printed by Gaulon, Bordeaux
Samuel P. Avery Fund 1921.10657

78.
Francisco Goya
(Painter and printmaker)
Spanish, 1746–1828
Bullfight in a Divided Arena, 1825
Crayon lithograph with scraping
12 x 16⅜ in.
Printed by Gaulon, Bordeaux
Samuel P. Avery Fund 1921.10658

79. (plate 50)
Francisco Goya
(Painter and printmaker)
Spanish, 1746–1828
Bravo Toro (Picador Caught by a Bull), 1825
Crayon lithograph with scraping
12¼ x 16¼ in.
Printed by Gaulon, Bordeaux
Samuel P. Avery Fund 1921.10656

80.
Francisco Goya
(Painter and printmaker)
Spanish, 1746–1828
The Famous American, Mariano Ceballos, 1825
Crayon lithograph with scraping
12¼ x 16 in.
Printed by Gaulon, Bordeaux
Samuel P. Avery Fund 1921.10655

81. (plate 52)
Eugène Delacroix
(Painter and printmaker)
French, 1798–1863
Wild Horse Brought Down by a Tiger, 1828
Lithograph: crayon, brush and scraping; early proof before letters
8⅜ x 10½ in.
Probably printed by C. Motte, Paris
Gift of W.G. Russell Allen 1960.262

82. (plate 51)
Luigi Sabatelli
(Painter and printmaker)
Italian, 1772–1850
The Bear Hunter, about 1820
Inspired by a passage from Ariosto's epic poem, *Orlando Furioso*, Canto 19
Crayon lithograph with scraping, on thin gray paper mounted during printing
9 x 12 in.
Printed by Vassalli, Milan
Katherine E. Bullard Fund in Memory of Francis Bullard 1995.456

83. (plate 17)
Théodore Géricault
(Painter, sculptor, and printmaker)
France, 1791–1824
Wagon Loaded with Wounded Soldiers, 1818
Crayon lithograph
11⅜ x 11⅝ in.
Printed by C. Motte, Paris
Fund in Memory of Horatio Greenough Curtis 1957.546

84.
Conrad Gessner
(Painter and printmaker)
Swiss, 1764–1826
Cavalry Charging, 1801
From *Specimens of Polyautography*, published by Ph. André, London, 1803
Pen lithograph, hand signed in pen in image
9 x 12½ in.
Gift of W.G. Russell Allen 1941.176

85.
Carle Vernet
(Painter and printmaker)
French, 1758–1836

Horse-Drawn Artillery Piece, 1818–20
Crayon lithograph
$9\frac{1}{8}$ x $16\frac{1}{2}$ in.
Printed by C. de Lasteyrie, Paris
Gift of W.G. Russell Allen 1938.617

86. (plate 16)
Antoine Pierre Mongin
(Painter, printmaker and writer)
French, 1762–1827
The Duel, 1818
Crayon lithograph
$11\frac{1}{4}$ x $15\frac{1}{4}$ in.
Printed by G. Engelmann, Paris
Lee M. Friedman Fund 1988.538

87.
Auguste Marie Raffet
(Painter and printmaker)
French, 1804–1860
Reveille, 1842
Crayon lithograph with scraping on thin cream paper mounted during printing
$7\frac{1}{2}$ x $9\frac{1}{4}$ in.
Printed by Auguste Bry and published by Gihaut frères, Paris
Harvey D. Parker Fund, 1913 M23376

88.
Auguste Marie Raffet
(Painter and printmaker)
French, 1804–1860
Nocturnal Review, 1836
Crayon lithograph with scraping on thin paper mounted during printing
$7\frac{7}{8}$ x $10\frac{3}{4}$ in.
Printed and published by Gihaut frères, Paris
Gift of Miss Ellen Bullard 1925.1244

89.
Carle Vernet
(Painter and printmaker)
French, 1758–1836
Mameluke with Rearing Horse, 1821
Crayon lithograph
$11\frac{1}{8}$ x $11\frac{3}{4}$ in.
Printed by F. Delpech, Paris
Willam A. Sargent Fund 1954.1049

90.
Nicholas Toussaint Charlet
(Painter and printmaker)
French, 1792–1845
Standing Turk, 1828
From a series of eighteen sketches in lithographic ink, *Croquis et pochades à l'encre par Charlet*
Lithograph: brush and crayon with scraping
$9\frac{7}{8}$ x $7\frac{1}{8}$ in.
Printed by Villain and published by Gihaut frères, Paris
Bequest of W.G. Russell Allen 1960.90

91.
Jean Antoine Gros
(Painter and printmaker)
French, 1771–1835
Chief of the Mamelukes on Horseback Signalling for Help, 1817
Other impressions included in the *Album lithographique* (see no. 108) published by F. Delpech, Paris, 1818
Crayon lithograph
$12\frac{5}{8}$ x $9\frac{1}{4}$ in.
Gift of W.G. Russell Allen 1939.548

92.
Louis François Lejeune
(Army general and amateur printmaker)
French, 1776–1848
Cossack, 1806
Crayon lithograph
$7\frac{5}{8}$ x $5\frac{1}{8}$ in.
Printed in the atelier of Theobald and Georg Senefelder, Munich
Gift of W.G. Russell Allen, 1938 M34699

93.
Bartolommeo Pinelli
(Painter and printmaker)
Italian, 1781–1835
Lucia's Mother Reproving her with a Glance for her Prodigality, 1830
Plate 5 from a series of scenes from Manzoni's novel *I Promessi Sposi* (*The Betrothed*)
Pen lithograph
$11\frac{3}{4}$ x $13\frac{1}{4}$ in.
Printed by Belle Arti, Rome
Katherine E. Bullard Fund in Memory of Francis Bullard 1995.443

94.
Alexander Orlowsky
(Painter and printmaker)
Polish (active in Russia), 1777–1832
Russian Village Dance, 1826–27
Crayon lithograph
12 x $15\frac{3}{8}$ in.
Printed by A. Pluchart, St. Petersburg
Gift of Samuel P. Avery, 1899 M13991

95. (plate 14)
Francisco Goya
(Painter and printmaker)
Spanish, 1746–1828
Woman Reading to Two Children, probably 1819–22
Crayon lithograph
$4\frac{7}{8}$ x $5\frac{1}{8}$ in.
Probably printed by José Maria Cardano at the Hydrographic Bureau, Madrid
Katherine E. Bullard Fund in Memory of Francis Bullard 1970.469

96.
Thomas Stothard
(Painter, illustrator, and printmaker)
English, 1755–1834
The Lost Apple, 1803
From *Specimens of Polyautography*, second issue, published by G.J. Vollweiler, London, 1806
Pen lithograph
$12\frac{3}{4}$ x 9 in.
Gift of W.G. Russell Allen 1941.159

97.
Jean Henri Marlet
(Painter and printmaker)
French, 1771–1847
The Drawing Academy, from *Tableaux de Paris*, 1820–24
Crayon lithograph with orange-brown tint stone
$6\frac{7}{8}$ x $10\frac{1}{4}$ in.
Gift of W.G. Russell Allen 1938.515

98.
Dominique Vivant Denon
(Art collector, writer, and amateur printmaker)
French, 1747–1825
The Artist Drawing a Portrait of a Woman, 1816
Crayon lithograph on gray-brown paper
$6\frac{1}{2}$ x $7\frac{3}{8}$ in.
Fund in Memory of Horatio Greenough Curtis Fund 1940.97

99. (plate 15)
D.J. Redman
(Lithographic printer and amateur printmaker)
English, active about 1807–1823
Woman Threading a Needle by Candlelight, about 1815
Crayon lithograph with scraping
7 x $6\frac{5}{8}$ in.
Gift of W.G. Russell Allen 1923.1334

100. (plate 35)
Honoré Daumier
(Painter, sculptor, and printmaker)
French, 1808–1879
Penelope's Nights, 1842
From the satirical series on antique history and mythology, *L'Histoire ancienne*, for *Le Charivari* (1841–43)
Crayon lithograph
9⅜ x 7½ in.
Printed by Aubert and published by Bauger & Aubert
Bequest of W.G. Russell Allen 1963.1746

101. (plate 34)
Pierre Narcisse Guérin
(Painter and printmaker)
French, 1774–1833
The Vigilant One, 1816
From a set of three allegories on the theme of young artists
Crayon lithograph
10⅝ x 7¾ in.
Printed by G. Engelmann, Paris
Harvey D. Parker Collection, 1897
P18076

102. (plate 39)
Giuseppe Longhi
(Painter and printmaker)
Italian, 1766–1831
Head of a Young Woman Wearing a Turban, 1808–12
Crayon lithograph touched with graphite pencil on the eyes, mouth, and hair, presumably by the artist
7⅜ x 6⅞ in.
Printed in Milan, probably by De Werz
Katherine E. Bullard Fund in Memory of Francis Bullard 1995.412

103. (plate 37)
Wilhelm Reuter
(Painter, lithographic printer, and printmaker)
German, 1768–1834
Head of a Bearded Man in Profile, 1818
Crayon lithograph on paper washed with yellow watercolor
8½ x 6⅜ in.
George Peabody Gardner Fund 1957.134

104.
Joseph Fischer
(Painter and printmaker)
Austrian, 1769–1822
Four Male Heads in Renaissance Dress (The Ages of Man), 1803
Crayon lithograph on dark cream paper
7⅜ x 12 in.
Probably printed by Ph. André, London
Gift of W.G. Russell Allen 1923.1333

105.
Francesco Hayez
(Painter and printmaker)
Italian, 1791–1882
Three Heads in Exotic Dress in Conversation, 1821
Crayon lithograph
6½ x 8½ in.
Printed in Milan
Katherine E. Bullard Fund in Memory of Francis Bullard 1995.340

106. (plate 36)
Andrea Appiani
(Painter and printmaker)
Italian, 1754–1817
Head of a Bearded Man, 1808–12
Crayon lithograph in brownish ink
6½ x 1¼ in.
Probably printed by De Werz, Milan
Katherine E. Bullard Fund in Memory of Francis Bullard 1995.201

107.
Francesco Hayez
(Painter and printmaker)
Italian, 1791–1882
Sketch of Male Nude Holding a Sword and Bust of a Bearded Patriarch, 1821
Crayon lithograph
6 x 5¼ in.
Printed in Milan
Katherine E. Bullard Fund in Memory of Francis Bullard 1995.339

Case

108.
Louis Hippolyte Lebas
(Architect and printmaker)
French, 1782–1867
Antique Architectural Fragments
In *Album lithographique*, Paris, 1819
Crayon lithograph
6⅞ x 10¼ in.
Printed and published by F. Delpech
Gift of Paul J. Sachs and W.G. Russell Allen 1942.619

109.
Gaetano Canuti
(Printmaker)
Italian, active 1820s and 1830s
Amaryllis (pink)
In Canuti's album of fifty lithographs of flowers, *Collezione di cinquanta fiori scelti, disegnati in litografia*, Bologna, 1826
Crayon lithograph
12½ x 6⅞ in.
Printed by Bertinazzi, Bologna
Katherine E. Bullard Fund in Memory of Francis Bullard 1995.235

110. (plate 11)
Horace Vernet
(Painter and printmaker)
French, 1789–1863
The Young Widow
In *Fables choisies de La Fontaine*, vol. 2, Paris, 1818
Illustrated by Carle and Horace Vernet and Hippolyte Lecomte
Crayon lithograph
7½ x 9½ in.
Printed by G. Engelmann, Paris
Gift of Mrs. Samuel Cabot 1957.2206

111. (plate 42)
Thomas Barker (Barker of Bath)
(Painter and printmaker)
English, 1769–1847
A Study from Hampton-Down, near Bath
In *Thirty Two Lithographic Impressions from Pen Drawings of Landscape Scenery by Thomas Barker*, Bath, 1814
Pen lithograph
12⅞ x 9¼ in.
Printed under the direction of Barker by D. Redman
Fund in Memory of Horatio Greenough Curtis 1950.3598

112.
Heinrich von Rapp
(Banker, patron of the arts, and amateur printmaker)
German, 1761–1832
Bathers in a Woodland Pond, 1807
In Rapp, *Das Geheimnis des Steindrucks in seinem ganzen Umfange practisch und ohne Rückhalt nach eigenem Erfahrungen beschrieben von einem Liebhaber* (The Secret of Stone-Printing), published by J.G. Cotta, Tübingen, 1810
Pen lithograph
7½ x 9⅛ in.
Gift of Sylvester Rosa Koehler, 1898
K612